LACE KNIT SHAWLS, SWEATERS, SOCKS & HATS

STACKPOLE BOOKS

An imprint of Globe Pequot, the trade division of
The Rowman & Littlefield Publishing Group, Inc.
4501 Forbes Blvd., Ste. 200
Lanham, MD 20706
www.rowman.com

Distributed by NATIONAL BOOK NETWORK
800-462-6420

EMF

Copyright © 2021   Edition Michael Fischer GmbH,
www.emf-verlag.de
This edition of *Japanische Muster Stricken* first published in Germany by Edition
Michael Fischer GmbH in 2021 is published by arrangement with Silke Bruenink
Agency, Munich, Germany.

Cover: Meritt Hettwer and Amanda Wilson
Images: © Corinna Brix, München; © iravgustin/shutterstock (page 149); ©
Chapter illustrations: burao_sato/shutterstock
Project management: Isabella Krüger
Editing: Regina Sidabras, Berlin, Germany
Layout and Typesetting: Zoe Mitterhuber
Translation: Katharina Sokiran

British Library Cataloguing in Publication Information available

Library of Congress Cataloging-in-Publication Data
Names: Freyer, Birgit, 1962– author.
Title: Lace knit shawls, sweaters, socks & hats : 26 designs inspired by
    Japanese stitch patterns / Birgit Freyer.
Description: Lanham, MD : Rowman & Littlefield Publishing Group, [2022] |
    Summary: "The 26 knitted lace patterns in this book are designed to
    showcase your stitches in pieces that can be worn anywhere. They
    incorporate Japanese lace stitch patterns to beautiful effects in
    pullovers, socks, shawls, hats, mitts, and more, in infinitely wearable
    patterns"— Provided by publisher.
Identifiers: LCCN 2022001231 (print) | LCCN 2022001232 (ebook) | ISBN
    9780811770989 (cloth) | ISBN 9780811770996 (epub)
Subjects: LCSH: Knitted lace—Patterns. | Knitting—Japan. | Knitwear.
Classification: LCC TT825 .F747 2022 (print) | LCC TT825 (ebook) | DDC
    746.2/26—dc23/eng/20220217
LC record available at https://lccn.loc.gov/2022001231
LC ebook record available at https://lccn.loc.gov/2022001232

First Edition

LACE KNIT SHAWLS, SWEATERS, SOCKS & HATS

26 Designs Inspired by
JAPANESE
STITCH PATTERNS

BIRGIT FREYER

Stackpole
Books
Essex, Connecticut
Blue Ridge Summit, Pennsylvania

Contents

Preface

How did I become enamored of Japanese stitch patterns? Frankly, I really only started to delve into Japanese stitch patterns in earnest at the beginning of 2020, when I was asked by the publisher to write this book. Although I had been given an English-language book of Japanese stitch patterns by a friend many, many years ago, at that time, I hadn't paid much attention to it. After the publisher's inquiry, I searched for, and found, the book and could immediately imagine what beautiful designs could be created featuring stitch patterns in the Japanese style.

For me, the signature look of Japanese-style designs is unusual lace patterns with prominent dynamics. I set to work immediately, designing many elegant lacy patterns in this style, which I am happy to present to you in this book.

With this book, I want to appeal to the experienced knitter as well as reach out to ambitious beginners, for whose benefit a chapter about knitting basics is included at the beginning.

The patterns are rated using three difficulty levels as follows:

毛糸 毛糸 毛糸 = little experience required

毛糸 毛糸 毛糸 = some practice is best

毛糸 毛糸 毛糸 = lace knitting experience a must

Enjoy your knitting!

Birgit Freyer

Basics

YARN

Yarns come in different weights and fiber compositions. When judging the thickness of a yarn (from super fine to bulky), yardage per weight is a good point for orientation. Yardage in this book is given in yards per 3.5 ounces (meters per 100 grams). Yarns with less yardage are generally thicker. The higher the yardage, the thinner the yarn will be. Yarns with a high yardage are very fine.

Knitting openwork designs with very fine yarns is often called "lace knitting." Yarns suitable for lace knitting have a yardage of 547 to 1,094 yards (500 to 1,000 meters) per 3.5 ounces (100 grams). Finer yarns produce an especially fine stitch definition. Working with them requires more knitting experience.

Yarn weight	Yardage per 3.5 oz (100 g)	Note
Fingering weight	up to 547 yd (500 m)	very suitable for beginners
Lace weight	547 yd (500 m) to 1,094 yd (1,000 m)	
Cobweb	more than 1,094 yd (1,000 m)	not suitable for beginners

Yarn can be composed of manmade, plant-based, or animal-derived fibers, as well as blends of these. For the finished item to be easily blockable and keep its shape later, the yarn should contain at least 75 percent natural fibers.

Unique among yarns are hairy yarns, such as mohair or brushed alpaca. In fabric knitted from these yarns, protruding hairs fill in the room between stitches, which creates a unique stitch definition and makes it possible to knit them at a looser gauge in a loftier way.

NEEDLE SIZE

For the needle size, "anything goes if it works for you" applies. To evaluate the stitch definition, a gauge swatch is necessary. Individual stitches should not be too large; the texture should still be recognizable. Lace shawls are worked with relatively large needles in relation to the yarn weight, using a needle size between US 6 and 8 (4.0 and 5.0 mm) for lace weight yarn. Loose knitters should use a smaller needle size, and tight knitters a larger needle size.

Note on project yardage: For designs with a specific stitch count, such as shawls and stoles, using a larger needle size will require a greater amount of yarn than listed for the sample. For measurement-oriented designs where no specific stitch counts are listed, such as sweaters and cardigans, choosing a larger needle size will decrease the total yardage needed as compared to the sample.

GAUGE SWATCH

Swatching for gauge is always necessary to determine the correct needle size for every project. If the gauge swatch turns out too tight (has more stitches than the sample), a larger needle size than listed should be used. The gauge swatch should always be worked in the same stitch pattern as the intended project.

Please note: Knit and purl stitches should always be worked at the same tension. If this should prove to be difficult to achieve, using an interchangeable needle system can help, working wrong size rows with a smaller or larger needle size as needed.

With some of the designs, a gauge swatch is also needed to determine correct stitch counts. This applies to accessories such as cowls and loops, arm warmers or fingerless gloves, as well as hats, which all require a certain circumference of the finished item for a proper fit.

In the pullovers and the cardigan from this book, stitch counts are not determined through a gauge swatch. For these garments, increases are worked until the listed measurement has been reached for the proper size.

The gauge swatch should be washed and then spread out horizontally until completely dry. For lace patterns, the gauge swatch will need to be blocked (see "Blocking Lace" on page 17). Lace patterns will develop their whole beauty only after blocking.

MY GRANDMOTHER'S TIP
"Always keep the gauge swatch, and wash it together with the project every time. This way, it will continue to have the same color as the actual project and can be used for mending when needed."

CASTING ON

There are different ways to cast on stitches. Some cast-on methods produce a tighter, others a more elastic, cast-on edge. The time-tested classic of all cast-ons is the long-tail cast-on.

Long-Tail Cast-On

This cast-on method creates a sturdy and elastic cast-on edge.

The long-tail cast-on is worked with either one or two needles. Since most knitters are prone to work this cast-on rather tightly, using two needles held parallel to each other will produce the best results.

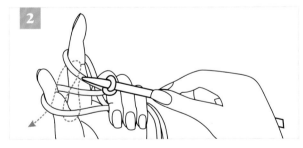

First, the yarn is fastened with a beginning slipknot, after having left a long beginning tail. Casting on 50 stitches will require a length of yarn about equal to the span of your outspread arms.

Place the yarn connected to the skein over your index finger, and the unattached yarn tail over the thumb. Lead the needle at the front (thumb) strand of the yarn from bottom to top; lead the needle at the third (index finger) strand of the yarn from top to bottom. Finally, lead the needle back from top to bottom between the two strands at the thumb.

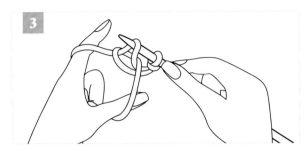

Drop the loop at the thumb, and tug at the yarn to tighten the loop on the needle.

Repeat Steps 2 and 3 until the required number of stitches has been cast on to the needle.

> **TIP**
> When casting on larger stitch counts, always count to 50, and then keep a tally on a sheet of paper. Alternately, you can place a stitch marker after every 50 stitches.

Crocheted Chain

Using a crocheted chain is convenient when casting on larger numbers of stitches. To crochet the chain, use a crochet hook in the same size as the knitting needles for the project.

First, crochet a chain. It should have at least the same number of chains as the number of stitches to be cast on. With your knitting needle and the project yarn, pick up and knit the stitches from the crocheted chain by inserting the knitting needle into one chain and then pulling the working yarn through. Repeat this process for every chain, until the required number of stitches has been cast on to the knitting needle. After this, knit as instructed.

Backward-Loop Cast-On

The backward-loop cast-on is convenient for casting on small numbers of stitches and bridging short distances, such as when working buttonholes. Casting on stitches using the backward-loop cast-on method should be considered an auxiliary cast-on when you have only one strand of working yarn at your disposal.

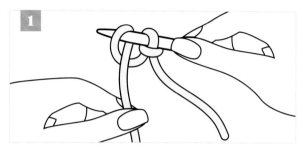

Using your thumb and index finger, twist the yarn into an e-loop, and place it onto the needle.

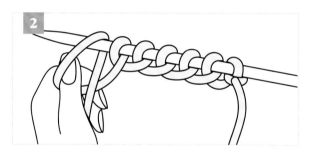

Repeat this process until the required number of stitches has been cast on.

TIPS & TRICKS

Lifeline

A lifeline (also called auxiliary line or safety line) is needed when a pattern has been knit without mistakes up to a point but you are unsure about the rows to be worked ahead.
The lifeline is inserted while you work.

The live stitches are on the cord of the circular needle. You can use a tapestry needle to thread a piece of contrasting color yarn through the live stitches.

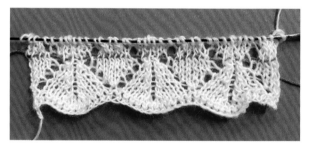

Alternately, you can attach the piece of contrasting color yarn directly to the needle. Some circular needles, such as those by Knitter's Pride, have ends on the needle tips that feature a practical small hole through which the lifeline can be inserted. This way, the stitches slide onto the lifeline by themselves.

Should you detect a mistake in your knitting later on, or need to make changes, just pull the knitting needles out of the live stitches of the last row, unravel the section down to the lifeline, and put the held stitches back on the needles.
You can remove and reinsert lifelines at various points as you work. You remove the lifeline a final time when it's no longer needed.

Joining New Working Yarn

As a general principle, new working yarn is always joined at the end of the row or in inconspicuous spots (such as under the arm). If the yarn is composed mostly of animal fiber, the ends can be felted onto each other. For this step, the ends need to be torn. Tearing off the ends rather than cutting them is important!

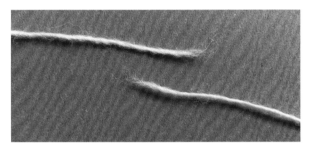

The two yarn ends are placed onto the palm, overlapping about 1 to 1.5 in (3 to 4 cm), moistened with a small amount of water, and rubbed together until the two strands have fused and dried.

If the yarn is composed mostly of silk, plant-based, or manmade fibers, the yarn ends can't be felted onto each other. For these, I recommend splitting the strands (untwist the old and new yarns and cut off a few inches of half the strands from both the old and the new yarns so that when worked together, they will be the same weight as one full strand).

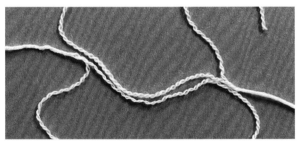

A few stitches are worked with half a strand each from the old skein and the new skein.
For knitted pieces worked in back-and-forth rows with turning, the last three stitches of the old row and the first three stitches of the new row should be worked with half a strand each from the old skein and the new one.

BINDING OFF

At the end of the work, stitches are bound off. This can be done using different methods.

Binding Off with Passing Over

Binding off with passing over is the easiest and most often used bind-off method.

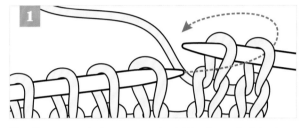

The first two stitches are worked. The first stitch is then passed over the second one.

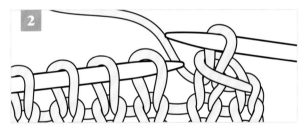

The next stitch is worked, and then the previous stitch is passed over this stitch.

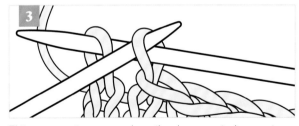

This process is repeated until only one stitch remains on the needle. Now the yarn tail is threaded through this last stitch to secure it.

> **TIP**
> Binding off sufficiently loosely can be challenging for some knitters. If this should apply to you, you can just use a larger needle size for binding off.

Elastic Bind-Off

For some of the patterns, such as arm warmers or fingerless gloves, it is recommended to bind off using an elastic bind-off method.

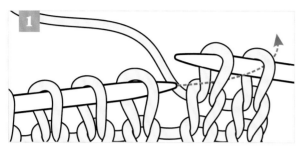

The first two stitches are knitted.

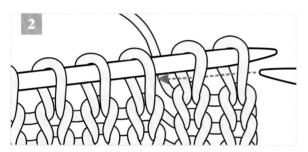

These two stitches are then returned to the left needle, and knitted together through the back loops.

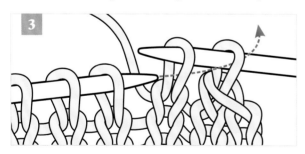

Now the next stitch is knitted. Both stitches are then returned to the left needle and knitted together through the back loops.

This process is repeated until only one stitch remains on the needle. Now the yarn tail is threaded through this last stitch to secure it.

Binding Off with a Crochet Hook

After the last wrong-side row (or stockinette stitch round), the live stitches of the knitted piece are bound off using a crochet hook. The crocheted bind-off is mostly used for lace patterns to prevent the bind-off edge from turning out too tight.
Stitches are bound off with a crochet hook during the last row of the chart. For this, the live stitches are crocheted off with one or three chains in between.

When you see this symbol ☐, you will crochet a chain into a live stitch of the knitted piece. For two or more stitches ⊢—⊣, according to the number shown in the box, you will crochet these off together. For this symbol ⊡, a chain of 3 is additionally worked between the single crochets.

The first stitch is lifted off with the crochet hook.

The working yarn is then pulled through the stitch slipped onto the crochet hook. This equals one crocheted chain.

The next stitch is lifted off with the crochet hook.

The working yarn is first pulled through one of the stitches. Then the working yarn is pulled through both stitches at once.

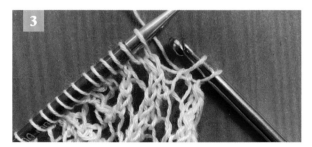

After this, another chain is crocheted.

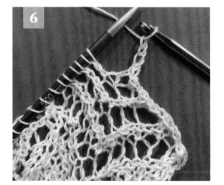

If instructions state to work 3 chains, the result will look like this.

In some spots, three stitches will be directly crocheted together:

Three stitches are slipped one after another.

The working yarn is first pulled through the three slipped stitches. After this, the working yarn is pulled through the two remaining stitches.

FINISHING

Adding Reverse Single Crochet Edging to Necklines and Edges

For an especially good-looking finish, such as around the neckline of a pullover or at the front edges of a cardigan, the knitted piece can be finished by working a row or round of reverse single crochet.

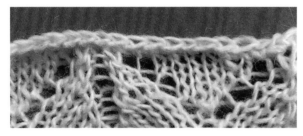

Here, first a row or round of regular single crochet is worked.

To work a single crochet, the crochet hook is inserted into the appropriate stitch, and the working yarn pulled through the stitch. There are two loops on the hook. Now the working yarn is pulled through both loops on the needle at once. A single crochet has been completed.

This is followed by a second row or round of reverse single crochet, this time in the opposite direction, working from left to right.

Sewing in Ends

After completing the knitting, all yarn ends must be woven in, preferably at the outside edge of the piece. Excess will be trimmed only after the piece has been washed and dried.

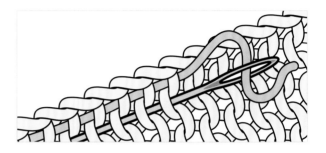

Washing and Blocking

After the ends have been woven in, the knitted piece needs to be washed in water with wool detergent—the ball band of the yarn will state whether to wash by hand or machine. If no specific washing instructions are given, always wash by hand.

Fill a basin with lukewarm water, and add a small amount of fiber-appropriate detergent. Let the knitted piece soak for half an hour. Yarns from mainly animal fiber in particular should not be agitated too much, to prevent accidental felting. Then press out excess liquid, and refill the basin with clear water to remove detergent residue. Finally, gently press out remaining water, and place the knitted piece on an even surface.

Pull the piece into the desired shape, and pin down wherever necessary.

Tip: Foam rubber mats from the toy store make a suitable blocking surface.

IMPORTANT
The knitted piece should be left
to dry at least two or three days!

Blocking Lace

Blocking improves the stitch definition and lets the lace pattern bloom. Shawls and scarves can be blocked to about 20 percent larger than their original size. In addition to a suitable blocking surface, you will need rustproof pins.

For pullovers and cardigans, spread out the garment on the blocking surface. Lightly pull out corners, and pin them down using tailor pins.

To block shawls, scarves, and stoles, blocking wires or thin metal rods from the hardware store can be used. Different shawl shapes are blocked in different ways.

Blocking a Boomerang-Shaped Shawl

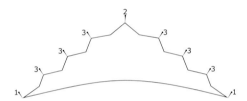

Spread out the boomerang-shaped shawl on the blocking surface. First, pin down the two tips with a tailor pin each (1). Now block the middle part (2). After this, pull out and pin down all other points evenly (3). Correct pin placement as needed.

Please note: Make sure that the center line is straight and both halves are symmetrical.

Blocking a Triangular Shawl

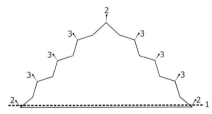

For a triangular shawl, first thread a piece of thin blocking wire through the yarn overs at the straight top edge at the shoulder side (1). Then pin down the three tips at the corners with tailor pins (2).

After this, pull out and pin down all other points evenly (3).

Correct pin placement as needed. The pulled-out points should be evenly spaced and all in one line. Distribute the stitches on the blocking wire evenly.

Blocking a Rectangular Stole

When blocking a stole that has been worked from the shoulder edge down, thread a thin blocking wire through the yarn overs at the straight top edge at the shoulder side (1). Then pin down all four corners with tailor pins (2). Finally, pull out and pin down all other points, evenly spaced (3).

Correct pin placement as needed. All points should be aligned in one line. Distribute the stitches on the blocking wire evenly.

Blocking a Scarf

For a scarf with two straight long edges, use two blocking wires, threading them through the yarn overs on the long sides (1). Then pin down all four corners with tailor pins (2).

Finally, pull out and pin down the points along the short sides, evenly spaced (3). Correct pin placement as needed.

All points should be aligned in one line. Evenly distribute the stitches on the blocking wire.

SPECIAL STITCHES

Increases from the Bar between Stitches (make 1)

⌧ Increases from the bar between stitches are also known as invisible increases since they are barely noticeable.

There are two different types of increases from the bar between stitches: the left-leaning and the right-leaning types. In both cases, the bar between stitches from the previous row or round is lifted onto the left needle and worked as a stitch.

Which one of the two methods to use depends on personal preference; however, the same method should always be used throughout the whole knitted piece.

For increases in both directions (such as along the center spine of a triangular shawl), to the right (before) the increase line, a right-leaning increase should be worked, and to the left of (after) it, a left-leaning one.

Left-Leaning Increase

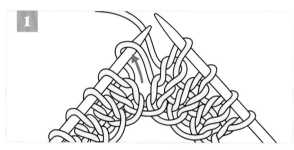

The bar between stitches from the previous row or round is lifted onto the left needle, inserting the left needle from front to back under the bar between stitches.

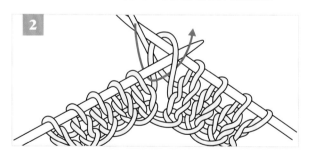

The bar is knitted through the back loop (twisted).

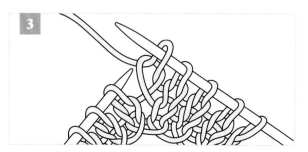

One stitch has been increased.

Right-Leaning Increase

The bar between stitches from the previous row or round is lifted onto the left needle, inserting the left needle from back to front under the bar between stitches.

The bar is knitted through the front loop.

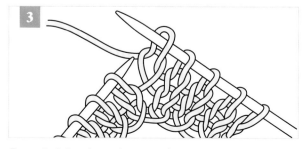

One stitch has been increased.

Making 2 Stitches from 1 (kfb increase)

▽ Two stitches are made out of one.

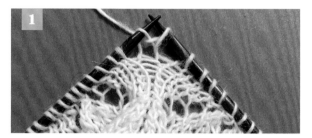

Knit one stitch, keeping the old stitch on the left needle.

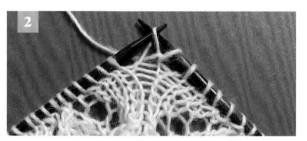

Knit this stitch a second time, this time knitting through the back loop (through the back leg of the stitch, twisted).

This is how the two new stitches will look.

Making 2 Stitches from 3

▽ Two stitches are made out of originally three.

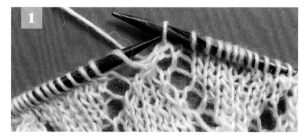

First, knit two stitches together.

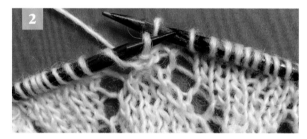

Now return the second one of the two stitches to the left needle, inserting the needle from back to front.

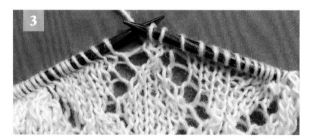

Knit this stitch together with the next one on the left needle as "slip-slip-knit."

Making 2 Stitches from 2

◆ Two stitches are knitted into two stitches as follows:

1. Knit two stitches together, keeping the old stitches on the left needle.
2. Knit these two stitches together a second time, this time, left-leaning as "slip-slip-knit."

To explain: This process works the same as V making 2 stitches from 1 but makes 2 stitches at the same time.

Knitting through the Back Loop

⧜ When knitting a stitch through the back loop, the stitch is twisted around itself once.

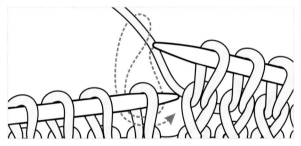

The working yarn is located behind the work. Insert the right needle through the back leg of the stitch (to twist the stitch), and pull the working yarn through.

Making 3 Stitches from 3

⎑⎐⎑ Three stitches are knitted into three stitches as follows:

Pass the third stitch on the left needle over the two preceding stitches.

After this, knit one stitch, make a yarn over, and then knit another stitch.

TIP
To avoid unsightly holes in the knitted fabric, yarn overs should always be worked twisted in the following row or round.

READING CHARTS

Knitting Charts Compared to Written-Out Instructions

After a short learning period, knitting from a chart will be faster and easier than knitting from instructions written out row by row. Knitting charts show in a simple and concise form how the pattern should be worked. With some practice, a knitting chart can be read like a picture book.

Most stitch patterns are created while working a right-side row (RS) or, when working in the round, the first one of two rounds, the "pattern row" or "pattern round." When working in rows, the stitches in the immediately following wrong-side row (WS) are usually purled; when working in the round, the stitches in the immediately following round are usually knitted.

Knitting charts are to be read in the direction of the actual knitting, from right to left and from bottom to top. In this book, wrong-side rows and even-numbered rounds are not shown in the charts, since all stitches are to be worked as they appear (knit stitches knitted, and purl stitches purled).

In the following example, a small stitch pattern worked in back-and-forth rows will be explained.

The chart below shows a simple lace pattern with a pattern repeat 17 stitches in width and 14 rows in height.

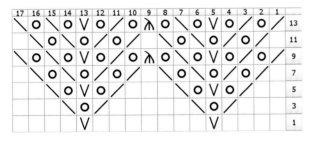

Written-Out Instructions for Comparison

Row 1 (RS): Knit 4 stitches, kfb, knit 7 stitches, kfb, knit 4 stitches.
Row 2 (WS): Purl all stitches. (This row and all following even-numbered rows are not shown in the chart.)
Row 3: Knit 3 stitches, k2tog, 1 yarn over, skp, knit 5 stitches, k2tog, 1 yarn over, skp, knit 3 stitches.
Row 4: Purl all stitches.
Row 5: Knit 2 stitches, k2tog, 1 yarn over, kfb, 1 yarn over, skp, knit 3 stitches, k2tog, 1 yarn over, kfb, 1 yarn over, skp, knit 2 stitches.
Row 6: Purl all stitches.
Row 7: Knit 1 stitch, k2tog, 1 yarn over, k2tog, 1 yarn over, skp, 1 yarn over, skp, knit 1 stitch, k2tog, 1 yarn over, k2tog, 1 yarn over, skp, 1 yarn over, skp, knit 1 stitch.
Row 8: Purl all stitches.
Row 9: K2tog, 1 yarn over, k2tog, 1 yarn over, kfb, 1 yarn over, skp, 1 yarn over, sk2p, 1 yarn over, k2tog, 1 yarn over, kfb, 1 yarn over, skp, 1 yarn over, skp.
Row 10: Purl all stitches.
Row 11: Knit 1 stitch, k2tog, 1 yarn over, k2tog, 1 yarn over, skp, 1 yarn over, skp, knit 1 stitch, k2tog, 1 yarn over, k2tog, 1 yarn over, skp, 1 yarn over, skp, knit 1 stitch.
Row 12: Purl all stitches.
Row 13: K2tog, 1 yarn over, k2tog, 1 yarn over, kfb, 1 yarn over, skp, 1 yarn over, sk2p, 1 yarn over, k2tog, 1 yarn over, kfb, 1 yarn over, skp, 1 yarn over, skp.
Row 14: Purl all stitches.

In this example, one can clearly see that the more that happens during the pattern row, the longer and more convoluted the written-out instructions will become. Furthermore, the flow of the pattern is not easily recognizable.

The two symbols ⟋ and ⟍ in the chart stand for decreases, which have a certain direction and are leaning toward a destination. This corresponds to what can be seen in the actual knitted piece.
The action from some of the symbols, such as V̄, results in 2 stitches. This means that in the following wrong-side row, there will be one stitch more. In most cases, this additional stitch will be canceled out by a decrease in the next pattern row.

Widthwise and Heightwise Pattern Repeats

If within a knitted piece, groups of stitches are to be repeated widthwise and/or heightwise, these will be shown in the form of pattern repeats, which have to be repeated as stated in the instructions.
The following chart shows one example each for a heightwise pattern repeat and a one-time widthwise repeat.
The stitches before and after the widthwise pattern repeat are worked only once each.

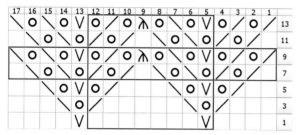

The heightwise pattern repeat shows which group of stitches to stack on top of each other. In the example shown, Rows 7 through 10 are repeated multiple times. For ease of reading, these rows are enclosed in a frame. After Row 10 (a wrong-side row to be purled) has been completed, work begins again at Row 7.
The widthwise pattern repeat shows which group of stitches to repeat within the same row. In the example shown, the group of stitches from 5 through 12 is worked multiple times in this row.
After having worked stitch 12, work begins again from stitch 5. For ease of reading, these stitches are framed.

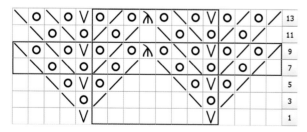

When, for this example, the widthwise pattern repeat (8 stitches wide) is worked 5 times total, this will yield 40 stitches, plus 4 stitches at the beginning and 5 stitches at the end of the row. There will be 49 stitches total in this row.
In the chart, only 17 stitches instead of the whole 49 are shown. To avoid confusion, stitches are not numbered within the row.

Working Lace Pattern Inserts

Some of the shawls feature a lace section. For the lace section to look best, the stitch count must be increased in these spots because the lace pattern pulls in. To keep the charts uncluttered, additional charts are often used for the separate lace inserts.

Rows 1 through 9 in the following example depict the main chart.

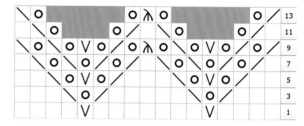

From Row 11 on, the lace insert begins. The symbol V in Row 9, which is shown in both charts, serves as a point of reference.
The smaller chart must be mentally built in to the main chart (gray areas).

From Row 11 on, both charts are used alternately. Start with the first 3 stitches from the top chart; then 5 stitches from the bottom chart and then again 5 stitches from the top chart are to be worked, etc.

It is also possible to incorporate the lace insert directly into the larger chart, which would look like this:

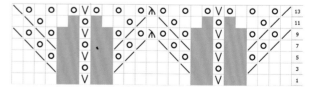

Especially with larger items, this way of charting can quickly become very unwieldy, and it takes up much more space. This example demonstrates how the gray box ▓ is a special case. In this spot, there is no stitch to be worked. The box is just a placeholder, to keep the chart less cluttered.

KNITTING SYMBOL EXPLANATIONS

This overview explains all symbols used in the knitting charts in this book.

▨ No stitch; no action required. This symbol is used as placeholder only.

☐ Knit stitch. Knit the stitch in all rows or rounds.

~ Knit stitch. When working in rows, knit this stitch in right- and wrong-side rows, and when working in rounds, purl this stitch in even-numbered rounds.

ᛤ Knit stitch. When working in rows, knit this stitch through the back loop in wrong-side rows, and when working in rounds, purl this stitch through the back loop in even-numbered rounds.

● Purl stitch. Purl the stitch in all rows or rounds.

Σ Selvedge stitch. Knit the first stitch of the row through the back loop. Slip the last stitch of the row purlwise, with yarn in front of work.

O Yarn over. Place the yarn from front to back over the needle once. When working in rows, purl the yarn over in the following wrong-side row, and when working in rounds, knit it in the following round.

Ⴝ Increase from the bar between stitches. Increase one stitch by lifting the bar between stitches onto the needle and then knitting it through the back loop (twisted).

╱ Knit 2 stitches together (k2tog). Insert the needle from left to right through 2 stitches at once, and knit them as one.

⟋ Knit 3 stitches together (k3tog). Insert the needle from left to right through 3 stitches at once, and knit them as one.

Ⱥ Knit 4 stitches together (k4tog). Insert the needle from left to right through 4 stitches at once, and knit them as one.

╲ Knitting 2 stitches together with passing over (skp). Slip 1 stitch knitwise, knit 1 stitch, pass the slipped stitch over the knitted one.

λ Knitting 3 stitches together with passing over (sk2p). Slip 1 stitch knitwise, k2tog, pass the slipped stitch over the stitches knitted together.

ᐱ Knitting 4 stitches together with passing over (sk3p). Slip 1 stitch knitwise, knit 3 stitches together, pass the slipped stitch over the stitches knitted together.

Λ Centered double decrease (cdd). Slip 2 stitches together knitwise, knit 1 stitch, pass the slipped stitches over the knitted one.

╱• Purl 2 stitches together (p2tog). Insert the needle from right to left through 2 stitches at once, and purl them as one.

V Knit front and back (kfb). Knit the same stitch first through the front loop, and then again through the back loop.

▽ Making 2 stitches from 3 (2from3). Knit 2 stitches together, place the second stitch back onto the left needle, slip this stitch knitwise, slip the next stitch knitwise, place both stitches back onto left needle and knit them together through the back loop.

◆ Making 2 stitches from 2 (2from2). Knit 2 stitches together, but leave the stitches on the left needle, and then slip each of these stitches knitwise one at a time, place them back on the left needle, and knit them together through the back loop.

② 2 yarn overs. In the following wrong-side row, work "purl 1, knit 1" into the double yarn over.

③ 3 yarn overs. In the following wrong-side row, work "purl 1, knit 1, purl 1" into the triple yarn over.

⊐o⊑ Making 3 stitches from 3 (3from3). Pass the third stitch on the left needle over the first two stitches; knit 1 stitch, 1 yarn over, and then knit 1 stitch.

⟍⟍ Cable. Hold 2 stitches on a cable needle behind work, knit the next 2 stitches on the main needle, and then knit the 2 stitches from the cable needle.

⁖ When working crocheted bind-off, this symbol means to chain 3 between bind-off stitches.

⊢─┤ When working crocheted bind-off, combine the number of stitches in the box into 1 stitch (as described on pages 14–15).

SOCK KNITTING WORKSHOP

Round Wedge Heel

Heels can be worked many different ways. My favorite one is the Round Wedge Heel. Ever since I learned this heel type, sock knitting has been much more fun to me. This heel has the advantage of having a nicely rounded shape, fitting well, and being a pleasure to knit.
The heel portion is worked over half of the stitches of the round, so the stitch pattern can be continued uninterrupted on the top of the foot.

To work a Round Wedge Heel, besides knit and purl stitches, German short rows involving turning stitches are required.

When turning using the German short row method, the turning stitch is first slipped purlwise with working yarn in front of work.

Then the working yarn is pulled toward the back over the right needle so two legs of the stitch sit on the needle (a double stitch).

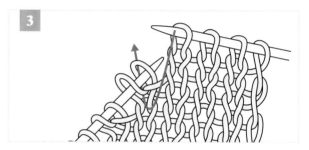

When returning to this spot later to work the turning stitch, the double stitch is treated and counted as one stitch, either knitting or purling both legs together as per instructions.

Example for a sock with 64 stitches:
Half of the stitches are used for the heel = 32 stitches. First, knit these 32 stitches. Now turn with a double stitch, and then purl 30 stitches. Turn again with a double stitch, and now knit 28 stitches. Continue to work in this manner, always working 2 stitches fewer in every row, until only 4 stitches remain on the needle.

> **PLEASE NOTE**
> Depending on the overall stitch count, shorten your rows to a final 4 to 8 stitches.

Now that the first heel wedge is finished, work one or two rounds over all stitches again. Then work short rows again for the second heel wedge. After having worked one or two additional rounds, work short rows a third time. When working over all stitches, continue the stitch pattern on the top of the foot.

Toe Decreases

To shape the toe section, you will now decrease at the outsides of both the top of the foot and the sole. This will amount to 4 decreases each in the 1st, 3rd, 5th, and 7th rounds. After this, decreases will be worked in every round, until only 16 stitches remain on the nee-dles. In the last round, work decreases of 3 stitches to 1 as shown in the chart below.

The last remaining 8 stitches will be cinched as follows: Break the working yarn, thread the end through a tapestry needle, and pull it through the last 8 stitches. Weave in the yarn tail.

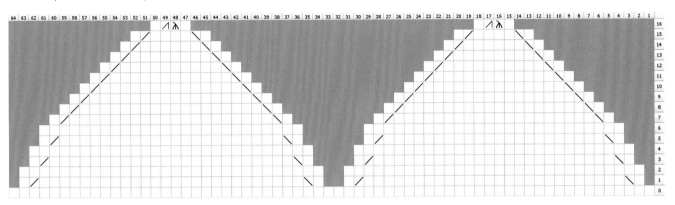

KNITTING PATTERNS FROM THIS BOOK

The knitted items featured in this book are adjustable to any size. For accessories, a widthwise pattern repeat can be additionally worked or omitted. As an alternative, the needle size can be switched to a smaller or larger one. The sweaters and the cardigan in this book are worked in a top-down raglan construction, starting at the neck and working down to the hem. In the upper section of the yoke, increases are worked until the required circumference has been reached. More about this will be explained in the instructions for each pattern.

Most of the designs from this book can be modified. For instance, the Suyala Poncho can be worked in three options. The Kisaki Cardigan, presented as top-down raglan here, can be turned into a pullover.

Long infinity scarf patterns can be made into smaller cowls or arm warmers by reducing the stitch count. Vice versa, cowls can be turned into long, looping scarves by increasing the stitch count. More detailed modifying instructions are provided in each pattern.

Take the Right Measurements

It is advisable to wear a thin, tightly fitting top when taking your measurements to determine size. Width/circumference are the most important. Length and arm length do not need to be measured, because you can try on the knitted piece as you go to get the desired fit.

KEEP IN MIND
that knitted pieces with lots of yarn overs (i.e., lace patterns) may grow lengthwise when worn, especially when worked in heavier yarns such as cotton, linen, and silk. For this reason, items in lace patterns should be worked aiming at more width than length.

Patterns

Yoshiko Hat

Knitting symbol explanations for the charts can be found on page 23.

DIFFICULTY LEVEL

毛糸 毛糸 毛糸

Finished Size

Height: 19.7 in (50 cm)
Circumference: 21.7 in (55 cm), adjustable

Materials

→ Lanartus Fine Merino Socks (75% merino wool fine, superwash, 25% polyamide; 459 yd/420 m, 3.5 oz/100 g per skein); 1 skein #100 White (approx. 197 yd/ 180 m, 1.5 oz/43 g needed)

→ Circular knitting needle, size US 4 to 6 (3.5 to 4.0 mm), 16 in (40 cm) long; or double-pointed needle set, size US 4 to 6 (3.5 to 4.0 mm)

Construction Note

The Hat is worked in the round, starting at the ribbed brim.

Gauge Swatch

Work the gauge swatch in back-and-forth rows with turning. Cast on 31 stitches and then continue from Gauge Swatch Chart. Only RS rows are shown in the chart. In WS rows, work all stitches as they appear (knit the knits and purl the purls, and purl the yarn overs). Repeat Rows 7 through 10 a total of 3 times. After Row 13, bind off all stitches loosely.

Wash the gauge swatch, and let it dry spread out flat. When dry, measure the width of the swatch. The section from stitch #4 through stitch #23 (denoted by arrows under the chart) should measure 3.1 in (8 cm) in width.

Gauge Swatch Chart

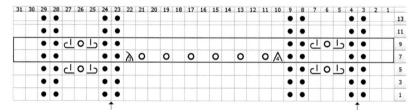

IF THE WIDTH DOES NOT MATCH
Adjust by using a smaller or larger needle size. However, if you like the stitch definition the original needle size gives and would like to keep it, you need to calculate a different stitch count.

EXAMPLE
The circumference should be approx. 21.7 in (55 cm). Your gauge swatch from stitch #4 through #23 measures 2.8 in (7 cm).
21.7 in (55 cm)/2.8 in (7 cm) = 7.75; rounded up to 8
8 x 2.8 in (8 x 7 cm) = 22.4 in (56 cm)
A repeat is 20 stitches.
8 x 20 stitches = 160 stitches

Hat Chart

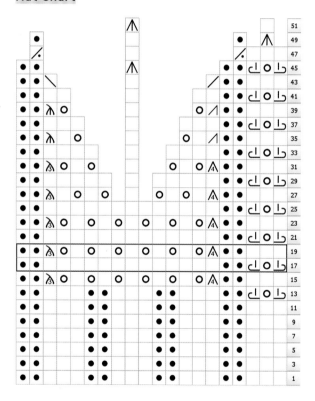

INSTRUCTIONS

Casting On and Working the Stitch Pattern

The Hat is worked in the round. Cast on 140 stitches (= approx. 21.7 in/55 cm), and join in the round. Continue from Hat Chart. Only pattern rounds are shown in the chart. In even-numbered rounds, work all stitches as they appear (knit the knits, and purl the purls), and knit the yarn overs. The chart shows one widthwise pattern repeat (20 stitches); work it 7 times around.

The framed area (Rounds 17 to 20) shows the height-wise pattern repeat. Repeat the heightwise pattern repeat until a height of 7.9 in (20 cm) has been reached, and then start crown decreases, working final Rounds 21 through 51 once. The total height of the hat is approximately 10 in (25 cm).
Cinch the last remaining 14 stitches: Break the working yarn, thread it through the remaining stitches, and weave in the end.

Finishing

After the ends have been woven in, soak the Hat in lukewarm water, gently press out excess water, and pull it into the finished shape.

Yoshiko Cowl

毛糸 毛糸 毛糸

Knitting symbol explanations for the charts can be found on page 23.

Finished Size

Width: 10 in (25 cm)
Circumference: 55.1 in (140 cm), adjustable

Materials

→ Lanartus Fine Merino Socks (75% merino wool fine, superwash, 25% polyamide; 459 yd/420 m per 3.5 oz/100 g); 2 skeins #100 White (approx. 656 yd/600 m, 5 oz/143 g needed)

→ Circular knitting needles, either size US 2.5 and 4 (3.0 and 3.5 mm) or US 4 and 6 (3.5 and 4.0 mm) (2 needle sizes are needed)

Construction Note

This Cowl is worked as a tube in the round and can be looped around the head/neck twice. The arrow in the schematic shows the direction of work.

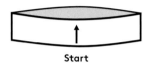

Start

Gauge Swatch

Work the gauge swatch in back-and-forth rows with turning. Cast on 31 stitches, and then continue from Gauge Swatch Chart. Only RS rows are shown in the chart. In WS rows, work all stitches as they appear (knit the knits and purl the purls), and purl the yarn overs. Repeat Rows 7 through 10 a total of 3 times. After Row 13, bind off all stitches loosely.

Wash the gauge swatch, and let it dry spread out flat. When dry, measure the width of the swatch. The section from stitch #4 through stitch #23 (denoted by arrows under the chart) should measure 3.1 in (8 cm) in width.

Gauge Swatch Chart

31	30	29	28	27	26	25	24	23	22	21	20	19	18	17	16	15	14	13	12	11	10	9	8	7	6	5	4	3	2	1	
		•	•				•	•														•	•				•	•			13
		•	•				•	•														•	•				•	•			11
		•	•	⊐	o	⊏	•	•														•	•	⊐	o	⊏	•	•			9
		•	•				•	•	⋋	o		o		o		o		o		o	⋌	•	•				•	•			7
		•	•	⊐	o	⊏	•	•														•	•	⊐	o	⊏	•	•			5
		•	•				•	•														•	•				•	•			3
		•	•				•	•														•	•				•	•			1

↑ (under stitch #23) ↑ (under stitch #4)

IF THE WIDTH DOES NOT MATCH

Adjust by using a smaller or larger needle size. However, if you like the stitch definition the original needle size gives and would like to keep it, you need to calculate a different stitch count.

EXAMPLE

The circumference should be approx. 55.1 to 57 in (140 to 145 cm).
Your gauge swatch from stitch #4 through #23 is 3.5 in (9 cm).
57 in (145 cm) / 3.5 in (9 cm) = 16.3, rounded down 16
16 x 3.5 in (9 cm) = 56 in (144 cm)
One widthwise pattern repeat will have 20 stitches.
16 x 20 stitches = 320 stitches

INSTRUCTIONS

Casting On and Working the Stitch Pattern

For casting on as well as working the first and last 10 rounds, the smaller needle size is used.

The Cowl is worked in the round. Cast on 360 stitches (= approx. 57 in/144 cm), and join in the round. For a cowl with smaller or larger circumference, cast on fewer or more stitches in increments of 20 (40, etc.). First, using the smaller needle size, work 10 rounds in garter stitch as follows: repeat "knit 1 round, purl 1 round" 5 times total.

After this, continue from Cowl Chart. Only pattern rounds are shown in the chart. In even-numbered rounds, work all stitches as they appear (knit the knits, and purl the purls), and knit the yarn overs.

The chart shows one widthwise pattern repeat (20 stitches); repeat it around as often as the stitch count permits.

Cowl Chart

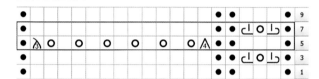

The framed area (Rounds 5 to 8) shows the heightwise pattern repeat. Repeat the heightwise pattern repeat until the desired size has almost been reached. After having completed Round 9, change to smaller needle size, and then work 10 rounds in garter stitch as follows: repeat "purl 1 round, knit 1 round" 5 times total. Then bind off all stitches, using the elastic bind-off method (see page 14).

Finishing

After the ends have been woven in, soak the Cowl in lukewarm water, gently press out excess water, and pull it into the finished shape.

Yoshiko Arm Warmers

Knitting symbol explanations for the charts can be found on page 23.

DIFFICULTY LEVEL

毛糸 毛糸 毛糸

Finished Size

Length: 13.8 in (35 cm)
Circumference: 9.5 in (24 cm), adjustable

Materials

→ Lanartus Fine Merino Socks (75% merino wool fine, superwash, 25% polyamide; 459 yd/420 m per 3.5 oz/100 g); 1 skein #100 White (approx. 284 yd/260 m, 2.2 oz/62 g needed)
→ Double-pointed needle set, US size 4 to 6 (3.5 to 4.0 mm)

Construction Note

These Arm Warmers or Fingerless Gloves are worked in the round.

Gauge Swatch

Work the gauge swatch in back-and-forth rows with turning. Cast on 31 stitches, and then continue from Gauge Swatch Chart. Only RS rows are shown in the chart. In WS rows, work all stitches as they appear (knit the knits and purl the purls), and purl the yarn overs. Repeat Rows 7 through 10 a total of 3 times. After Row 13, bind off all stitches loosely.

Wash the gauge swatch, and let it dry spread out flat. When dry, measure the width of the swatch. The section from stitch #4 through stitch #23 (denoted by arrows under the chart) should measure 3.1 in (8 cm) in width.

Gauge Swatch Chart

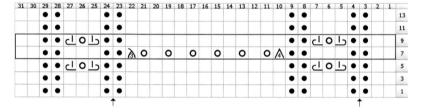

IF THE WIDTH DOES NOT MATCH OR A DIFFERENT WIDTH IS NEEDED
Adjust by using a smaller or larger needle size. However, if you like the stitch definition the original needle size gives and would like to keep it, you need to calculate a different stitch count.

EXAMPLE
The circumference should be approx. 12.6 in (32 cm). Your gauge swatch from stitch #4 through #23 measures 2.6 in (6.5 cm).
12.6 in (32 cm) : 2.6 in (6.5 cm) = 4.8, rounded up to 5
5 x 2.6 in (6.5 cm) = 13 in (32.5 cm)
One widthwise pattern repeat will have 20 stitches.
5 x 20 stitches = 100 stitches

INSTRUCTIONS

Casting On and Working the Stitch Pattern

Cast on 60 stitches, and join in the round. Now continue from Arm Warmer Chart. The widthwise pattern repeat in the chart is 20 stitches wide; work it 3 times around. Only pattern rounds are shown in the chart. In even-numbered rounds, work all stitches as they appear (knit the knits, and purl the purls), and knit the yarn overs.

First, work Rounds 1 through 16 once. Rounds 17 to 20 are the heightwise pattern repeat. Repeat the heightwise pattern repeat until the desired length has almost been reached. Finally, work Rounds 21 through 33 once.

After having completed Round 33, bind off all stitches, using the elastic bind-off method (see page 14).

Arm Warmer / Leg Warmer Chart

Finishing

After the ends have been woven in, soak the Arm Warmers in lukewarm water, gently press out excess water, and nudge them into their finished shape.

Yoshiko Leg Warmers

Knitting symbol explanations for the charts can be found on page 23.

DIFFICULTY LEVEL

毛糸 毛糸 毛糸

Finished Size

Length: 13.8 in (35 cm)
Circumference: 12.6 in (32 cm),
adjustable

Materials

→ Lanartus Fine Merino Socks (75%
  merino wool fine, superwash,
  25% polyamide; 459 yd/420 m
  per 3.5 oz/100 g); 1 skein #100
  White (approx. 383 yd/350 m,
  2.9 oz/83 g needed)
→ Double-pointed needle set, US
  size 4 to 6 (3.5 to 4.0 mm)

Construction Note

The Leg Warmers are worked in
the round.

INSTRUCTIONS

Casting On and Working the Stitch Pattern

Cast on 80 stitches, and join in the round. Work the same way as for
the Arm Warmers (using Arm Warmer / Leg Warmer Chart; see page
38). However, for the Leg Warmers, work the widthwise pattern repeat
of 20 stitches 4 times around.

OPTION
If the Leg Warmers are intended to be worn over ankle boots or booties,
they will fit best if the first and last few rounds are worked in
garter stitch. Additionally, these parts should be worked
with a smaller needle size (0.5 mm smaller).
Using the smaller needle size, cast on 80 stitches, and join in the round.
Now work 10 rounds in garter stitch as follows: repeat "purl 1 round, knit
1 round" 5 times total. After this, change to larger needle size,
and continue in stitch pattern, Rounds 17 through 20 of Arm Warmer /
Leg Warmer Chart from page 38. Finally, change back to smaller needle
size, and work 10 rounds in garter stitch as follows: repeat "knit 1 round,
purl 1 round" 5 times total.

OPTION
This photo shows the bootie option, which starts
and ends with garter stitch rounds (see page 40).

Airi Shawl

Knitting symbol explanations for the charts can be found on page 23.

DIFFICULTY LEVEL

毛糸 毛糸 毛糸

Finished Size

27.5 x 75 in (70 x 190 cm), adjustable

Materials

→ Coast Lacegarn from Filace by Birgit Freyer (55% merino wool, 45% cotton; 764 yd/698 m per 3.5 oz/100 g); 3 skeins (1.75 oz/ 50 g each) Ecru (approx. 875 yd/800 m, 4 oz/114 g needed, depending on finished size)
→ Circular knitting needle, US size 6 to 8 (4.0 to 5.0 mm)
→ Crochet hook in the same size

Gauge Swatch

For this pattern, a gauge swatch is not necessary since the main pattern is repeated until the desired size has almost been reached.

Construction Note

The Shawl is worked in one piece from the center out, starting in the middle of the top edge, as shown in the diagram.

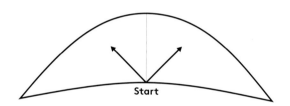

INSTRUCTIONS

Cast-On and Setup Rows
Cast on 9 stitches. In the following wrong-side row, and all other WS rows, purl all stitches. Chart A shows the complete Setup Rows section. Only RS rows are shown in the chart.

Main Part (Body of the Shawl)
Continue from Chart B, starting at Row 11. Rows 7/9, which have been worked in the previous chart, are shown here again for orientation—do not work them again.

Rows 11 through 22 are the heightwise pattern repeat and are worked 9 times total. The framed area shows the widthwise pattern repeat. With every repeat of the heightwise pattern repeat, the widthwise pattern repeat will be worked 3 times more. For a smaller/larger shawl, Rows 11 through 22 can be worked fewer/more times.

Transition to Edge
Continue from Chart C, starting with Row 23. Rows 19/21, which have been worked in the previous chart, are shown here again for orientation—do not work them again.
The framed area shows the widthwise pattern repeat. Work the widthwise pattern repeat as often as the stitch count permits.

Edge
Continue from Chart D, Row 37. Rows 33/35, which have been worked in the previous chart, are shown here again for orientation—do not work them again.
The framed area shows the widthwise pattern repeat. Work the widthwise pattern repeat as often as the stitch count permits.

In Row 51, the stitches are bound off with a crochet hook, with either 1 or 3 chains in between (see pages 14 and 15). This sometimes involves binding off a group of 3 stitches ⊢━━┥ together. For ⬚, a chain of 3 is worked between bound-off stitches.

Finishing
After the ends have been woven in, soak the Shawl in lukewarm water, gently press out excess water, and block it.

Chart A, Setup Rows

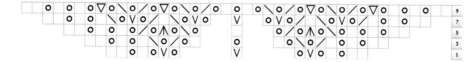

Chart B, Main Part

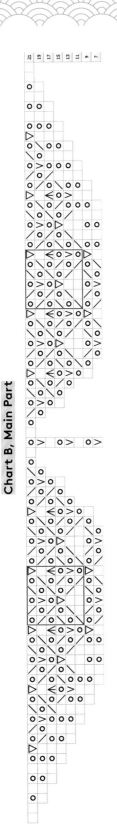

Chart C, Transition to Edge

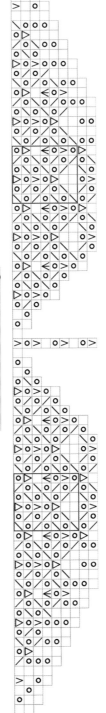

Chart D, Edge

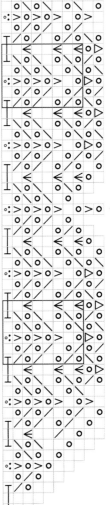

← Middle of shawl

Misaki Pullover

Knitting symbol explanations for the charts can be found on page 23.

DIFFICULTY LEVEL

毛糸 毛糸 毛糸

Finished Size

Adjustable; make to size desired as instructed.

Materials

→ BabyCotton from Filace by Birgit Freyer (100% cotton; 394 yd/360 m per 3.5 oz/100 g); in Perla, to-tal will depend on finished size: approx. 1,203 yd (1,100 m), 10.8 oz (306 g) for a long-sleeve sweater in size US 8/10; 1,312 yd (1,200 m), 11.8 oz (333 g) for size US 12/14 (yarn comes in 1.75 oz/50 g skeins, approx. 7 skeins for sizes above; estimate as needed for other sizes)

→ Circular knitting needle, US size 6 or 7 (4.0 or 4.5 mm)

→ Crochet hook in the same size

Please note: For a shorter pullover in size US 8/10, 6 skeins will be sufficient.

Gauge Swatch

For this pattern, a gauge swatch is not necessary since increases are worked until the desired size has been reached.

Construction Note

This sweater is worked in top-down raglan construction. All stitches (Sleeve – Front – Sleeve – Back) are cast on and worked together in one piece. The arrows in the schematic show the direction of work.

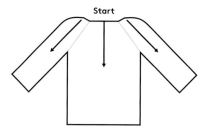

At the transitions between Sleeves and Body, in every other round, 2 stitches each are increased, meaning every other round will have 8 stitches more. The increases are accounted for in the chart.

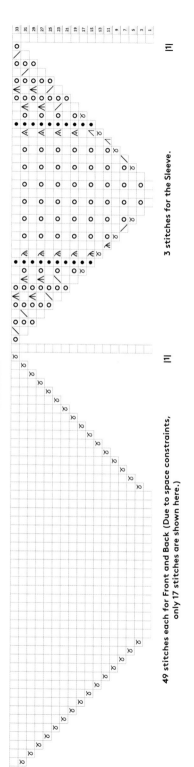

Chart A

33 31 29 27 25 23 21 19 17 15 13 11 9 7 5 3 1

|1|

3 stitches for the Sleeve.

|1|

49 stitches each for Front and Back (Due to space constraints, only 17 stitches are shown here.)

INSTRUCTIONS

Casting On & Yoke

Cast on 108 stitches. The number |1| indicates the raglan line stitch.

49		1		3		1		49		1		3		1	
Back	|1|	Sleeve	|1|	Front	|1|	Sleeve	|1|

Join in the round, and then knit for one round. Continue from Chart A. Only pattern rounds are shown in the chart. In even-numbered rounds, mostly knit stitches are worked—except for the sleeve, where the two purl stitches are purled in even-numbered rounds, too, and the yarn overs, knit.

Due to space constraints, only one Sleeve is shown, and the Body is shown only once, which means that the chart must be worked twice in each round.

> **PLEASE NOTE**
> It is strongly recommended that you mark each raglan line stitch with a stitch marker.

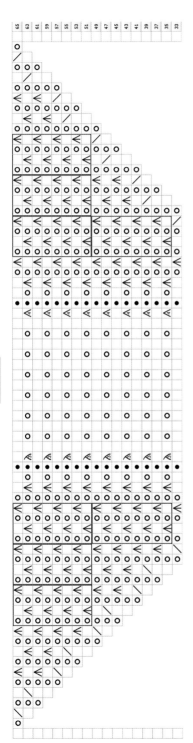

Chart B

Continue from Chart B (sleeve only), starting with Round 35. Round 33, which had been worked earlier, is shown here again for better orientation—do not work it again. Continue to work the Body sections in stockinette stitch as established, including right- and left-leaning increases.

Rounds 51 through 66 may be further repeated if the desired width has not yet been reached. With every repeat of Rounds 51 through 66, there will be four repeats of the widthwise pattern repeat (bold-framed area) more in the Sleeve section. For sizes 18 and larger, Rounds 51 through 66 should be repeated once more.

TIP
In regular intervals, a lifeline should be inserted (see page 12).

NOTE ABOUT LARGER SIZES
The raglan line (the 1 stitch between Body and Sleeves) for size US 12/14 should be approx. 10.6 in (27 cm) long. For larger sizes, this line will automatically become longer. However, the raglan line should not turn out too long, which would result in a too wide (and, therefore, too deep) armhole. If this is the case, a larger number of stitches (1 widthwise pattern repeat = 10 stitches more) can be cast on at the underarms using the backward-loop cast-on method. Details are provided in the next section.

CONTINUED

Main Part (Body)

After having completed Round 66, transfer the sleeve stitches to a stitch holder or piece of waste yarn for holding; they will be worked later. Add the raglan line stitches to the Body sections.

> **PLEASE NOTE**
> I recommend using a thick piece of yarn in a contrasting color for holding the sleeve stitches.

In place of the now-held sleeve stitches, cast on 13 new underarm stitches each between Front and Back as well as between Back and Front. The new overall Body stitch count is now a multiple of 16.

> **NOTE ABOUT LARGER SIZES**
> Instead of 13 stitches, either 29 or 45 underarm stitches can be cast on, to prevent the raglan line from becoming too long. In this case, later in the Sleeve Cap, two or four more repeats of the widthwise pattern repeat (of 16 stitches each) will be worked.

Continue Front and Back together in one piece in stockinette stitch in the round, until the desired length, minus approx. 5.9 in (15 cm) for the lace pattern, has been reached.

Edge

In Chart C, the widthwise pattern repeat is 16 stitches wide. Repeat it as often as the stitch count permits.

Chart C

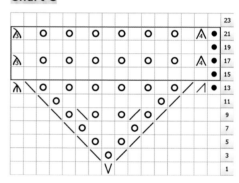

Work Rounds 15 through 22 a total of 3 times. After having completed Round 23, bind off all stitches loosely. Finish by adding a round of reverse single crochet (see page 16).

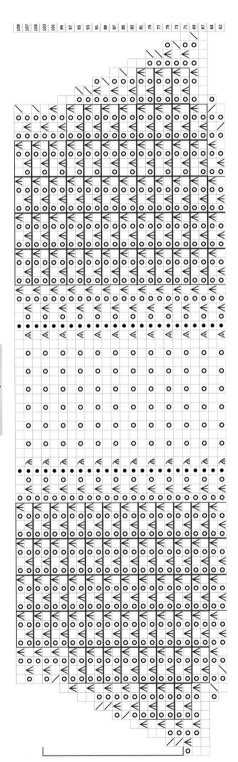

Chart D, Sleeve

Sleeve

The Sleeves are worked in the round. In even-numbered rounds, work all stitches as they appear (knit the knits, and purl the purls), and knit the yarn overs.

Take up the previously held sleeve stitches, and place them on the needle.

Additionally, work 13 stitches into the corresponding cast-on underarm stitches at the Body of the garment. The middle of the additionally cast-on underarm stitches will be the first stitch of the next round. (Please note for larger sizes: If, at the Body, 29 or 45 stitches had been previously cast on between Front and Back/ Back and Front instead, now work 29 or 45 stitches into them accordingly.)

Continue to work in the established pattern over the existing stitches.

Continue from Chart D with Round 67 as follows: Work 7 stitches into the corresponding cast-on underarm stitches, work over the formerly held sleeve stitches, 6 stitches into the corresponding cast-on underarm stitches.

Rounds 63/65, which have been worked earlier, are shown here again for orientation—do not work them again.

For sleeve tapering, in every 5th round, at the beginning and the end of the round, knit 2 stitches together each until the stitch count is again a multiple of 16, which can be either 48 or 64 stitches. For this, repeat Rounds 73 through 104.

After having completed Rounds 105/106, repeat Rounds 107 through 110 to the desired sleeve length, minus approx. 5.9 in (15 cm) for the sleeve cuff.

CONTINUED

Sleeve Cuff for 48 Stitches

Continue from Chart E, beginning with Round 111. Rounds 107/109, which have been worked in the previous chart, are shown here again for orientation—do not work them again.

Work Rounds 121 through 128 a total of 3 times. After having completed Round 129, bind off all stitches loosely.

Finish by adding a round of reverse single crochet (see page 16).

Chart E, Sleeve Cuff for 48 Stitches

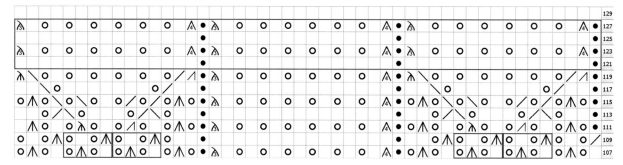

Sleeve Cuff for 64 Stitches

Continue from Chart F, beginning with Round 111. Rounds 107/109, which have been worked in the previous chart, are shown here again for orientation—do not work them again.

Work Rounds 121 through 128 a total of 3 times. After having completed Round 129, bind off all stitches loosely. Finish by adding a round of reverse single crochet (see page 16).

Chart F, Sleeve Cuff for 64 Stitches

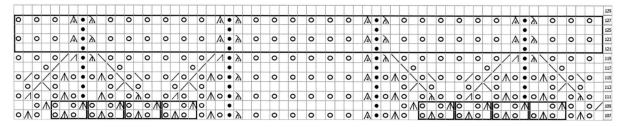

Finishing

Finish the neckline by adding a crocheted edging of 1 round of single crochet, followed by 1 round of reverse single crochet. After having woven in all ends, soak the Pullover in lukewarm water, gently press out excess water, and block to shape, lightly opening up the lace sections.

Misaki Pullover

Knitting symbol explanations for the charts can be found on page 23.

DIFFICULTY LEVEL

毛糸 毛糸 毛糸

Finished Size

Adjustable; make to size desired as instructed.

Material

→ Rhapsody from Filace by Birgit Freyer (100% silk; 546 yd/500 m per 3.5 oz/100 g); in Giallo, total depends on finished size: approx. 1,094 yd (1,000 m), 7 oz (200 g) for a short-sleeve sweater in size US 8/10; 1,203 yd (1,100 m), 7.8 oz (220 g) for size US 12/14 (yarn comes in 1.75 oz/50 g skeins; you will need 4 [5] skeins for sizes above; estimate as needed for other sizes)
→ Circular knitting needle, US 6 or 7 (4.0 or 4.5 mm)
→ Crochet hook in the same size

Gauge Swatch

For this pattern, a gauge swatch is not necessary since increases are worked until the desired size has been reached.

Construction Note

This sweater is worked in top-down raglan construction. All stitches (Sleeve – Front – Sleeve – Back) are cast on and worked together in one piece.

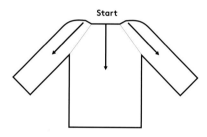

At the transitions between Sleeves and Body, in every other round, 2 stitches each are increased, meaning every other round will have 8 stitches more. The increases are accounted for in the chart.

INSTRUCTIONS

General Notes

Cast-on and Body for the short-sleeve sweater are worked the same as for the long-sleeve sweater (see pages 50–52).

For the Sleeves, Rounds 73 to 104 are not repeated. This means that Chart D (see page 53) for the Sleeve is worked only once. The chart automatically results in a stitch count that is a multiple of 16 at the end. Immediately after this, the Sleeve Cuff is worked, which has a widthwise pattern repeat of 16 stitches. Divide the total stitch count for the sleeve by 16. The result will be either an odd or an even number—follow the respective instructions.

Sleeve Cuff for Odd Number of Widthwise Pattern Repeats

For an odd result, such as 5 or 7 (= 80 or 112 stitches), the Sleeve Cuff is worked from Chart G1.

Continue with Round 111 of the chart.
Rounds 107/109, which have been worked earlier, are shown here again for orientation—do not work them again.
Sections framed in bold (stitches 1 through 16 and 33 to 48) show the respective widthwise pattern repeat, which is worked either 2 times (for 80 stitches) or 3 times (for 112 stitches).

Work Rounds 121 through 128 a total of 3 times. After having completed Round 129, bind off all stitches loosely.
Finish by adding a round of reverse single crochet (see page 16).

Chart G1, Sleeve Cuff for Odd Number of Widthwise Pattern Repeats

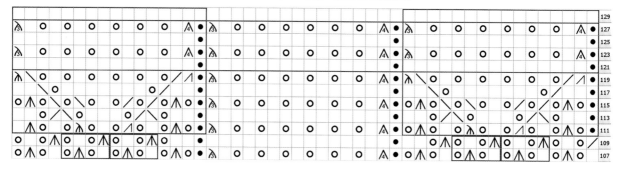

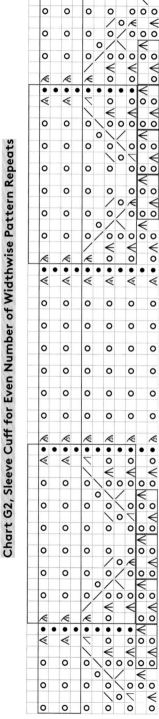

CONTINUED

Sleeve Cuff for Even Number of Widthwise Pattern Repeats

For a result of 4 (= 64 stitches), the Sleeve Cuff is worked from Chart F "Sleeve Cuff for 64 Stitches" (see Long-Sleeve Sweater from page 54).

For a different even-numbered result, such as 6 or 8 (= 96 or 128 stitches), the Sleeve Cuff is worked from Chart G2.

Continue with Round 111 of the chart.
Rounds 107/109, which have been worked earlier, are shown here again for orientation—do not work them again.
Sections framed in bold (stitches 9 through 24 and 41 through 56) show the respective widthwise pattern repeat, which is worked either 2 times (for 96 stitches) or 3 times (for 128 stitches).

Work Rounds 121 through 128 a total of 3 times. After having completed Round 129, bind off all stitches loosely. Finish by adding a round of reverse single crochet (see page 16).

Finishing

Finish the same way as for the Long-Sleeve Sweater (see page 54).

Chart G2, Sleeve Cuff for Even Number of Widthwise Pattern Repeats

Sachiko
Fingerless Gloves

Knitting symbol explanations for the charts can be found on page 23.

DIFFICULTY LEVEL

毛糸 毛糸 毛糸

Finished Size

Circumference: 6.3 in (16 cm)
Length: 7.1 in (18 cm)

Materials

→ Coast Lacegarn from Filace by
  Birgit Freyer (55% merino wool,
  45% cotton; 764 yd/698 m per
  3.5 oz/100 g); 1 skein (1.75 oz/
  50 g) Dove (approx. 164 yd/
  150 m, 0.74 oz/21 g needed)
→ Double-pointed needle set, size
  US 1 to 3 (2.25 to 3.25 mm)

Construction Note

The Fingerless Gloves are worked
in the round, either with or without a thumb gusset and thumb.

Gauge Swatch

Cast on 25 stitches, and work approx. 2.8 in (7 cm) in stockinette stitch in
rows (knit on RS, purl on WS).
Wash the gauge swatch, and let it dry spread out flat. When dry, measure
the width of the swatch. The whole swatch should be 3.1 in (8 cm) in
width. If the width does not match, use a smaller/larger needle size.

INSTRUCTIONS

Cast On

Cast on 50 stitches, and join in the round.
For smaller/larger arm warmers or fingerless gloves, cast on 2 or 4 stitches
fewer/more; these will fall on the Main Part (palm/back of the hand), not
the thumb.

CONTINUED

Right Fingerless Glove

Work from Chart A. Only pattern rounds are shown in the chart. In even-numbered rounds, work all stitches as they appear (knit the knits, and purl the purls), and knit the yarn overs.

Chart A, Right Fingerless Glove

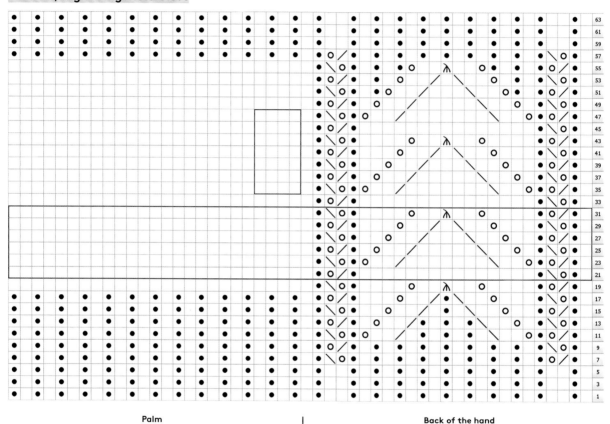

Palm | Back of the hand

The framed area (Rounds 21–32) shows the heightwise pattern repeat, which is worked 3 times. For longer arm warmers or fingerless gloves, the heightwise pattern repeat may be repeated once more. Adding a thumb is optional. In Rounds 35 to 48, 4 stitches are framed in bold, this is the thumb gusset placement. Before and after these 4 stitches, from Round 35 on, thumb gusset increases will be worked. Increase 1 stitch each from the bar between stitches as follows: ⌖.

Work the Thumb Gusset as Follows:

Round 35: ⌖, knit 4 stitches, ⌖.
Round 37: ⌖, knit 6 stitches, ⌖.
Round 39: ⌖, knit 8 stitches, ⌖.
Round 41: ⌖, knit 10 stitches, ⌖.
Round 43: ⌖, knit 12 stitches, ⌖.
Round 45: ⌖, knit 14 stitches, ⌖.
Round 47: ⌖, knit 16 stitches, ⌖.

After having completed Round 48, transfer the 18 thumb gusset stitches to a piece of waste yarn for holding.

For the Main Part, in Round 49, in the area of the Thumb Gusset, cast on 4 stitches by using the backward-loop cast-on method, and again join in the round. This returns the stitch count to the original number of 50 stitches. Continue to work from the chart. After having completed Round 63, bind off all stitches loosely.

Take up the 18 formerly held stitches again. At the transition to the Main Part, work 6 stitches into the corresponding stitches (= 24 stitches), and join in the round. Work "knit 1, purl 1" to the desired height, and then bind off the stitches either loosely or using the elastic bind-off method (see page 14).

Left Fingerless Glove

The Left Fingerless Glove is worked from Chart B the same way as the Right Fingerless Glove.

Chart B, Left Fingerless Glove

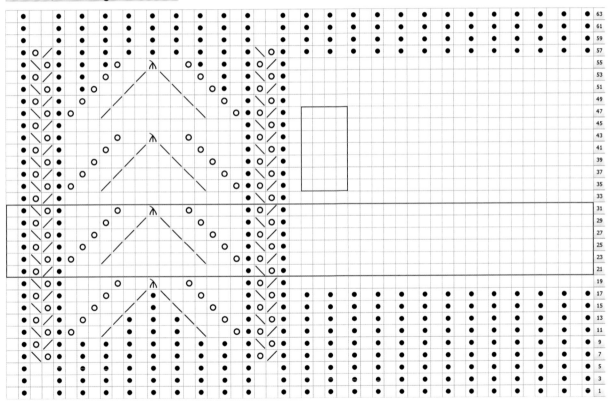

Back of the hand | Palm

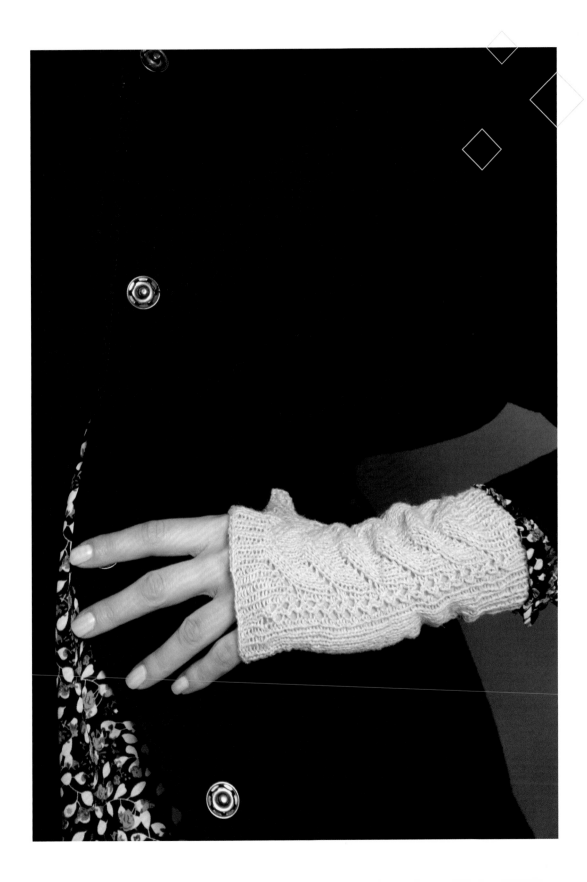

Jamini Socks

Knitting symbol explanations for the charts can be found on page 23.

Finished Size

US Women's 8.5–9.5, adjustable

Materials

→ Lang Yarns Jawoll (75% pure new wool, 25% polyamide, 459 yd/420 m per 3.5 oz/100 g); 2 skeins (1.75 oz/50 g each) #226 Silver (approx. 328 yd/300 m, 2.5 oz/71 g needed)

→ Double-pointed needle set, size US 1 (2.0 to 2.5 mm)

Construction Note

These Socks are worked in the round from the cuff down to the toe. Socks 1 and 2 are worked in reverse.

Gauge Swatch

For this pattern, a gauge swatch is not necessary.

INSTRUCTIONS

Cast-On & Leg – Socks 1 and 2

Cast on 72 stitches, and join in the round. For smaller/larger socks, cast on 9 stitches fewer/more.

Continue from Chart A. Only pattern rounds are shown in the chart. In even-numbered rounds, work all stitches as they appear (knit the knits, and purl the purls). Knit or purl the yarn overs through the back loop (twisted). From Round 19 on, in even-numbered rounds, work knit stitches and yarn overs through the back loop only.

CONTINUED

Chart A, Sock 1

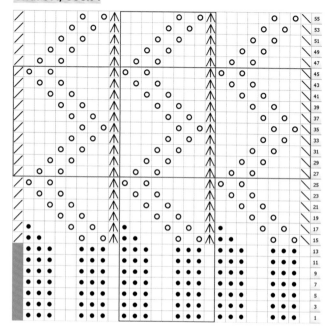

The narrow framed area (9 stitches wide) shows the width-wise pattern repeat. Work the widthwise pattern repeat 6 times around.

The wide framed area (Rounds 27 through 46) shows the heightwise pattern repeat. Work the heightwise pattern repeat 3 times.

Finally, work Rounds 47 through 56 once.

Throughout Rounds 15 through 55, always knit the first stitch of the round together with the last stitch of the old round.

Heel & Toe – Sock 1

Continue from Chart B, Sock 1, beginning with Round 57. Rounds 53/55, which have been worked in the previous chart, are shown here again for orientation—do not work them again.

Work the Heel, starting in Round 59 (framed round), in stockinette stitch, using your preferred method. If working a Round Wedge Heel, follow instructions on page 24.

Continue the stitch pattern on the top of the foot. In Rounds 67 through 86, repeat the stitch pattern on the top of the foot to the beginning of the toe decrease section. Work the toe decreases in stockinette stitch, using your preferred method. A technique tutorial for toe decreases is included on page 25 of this book.

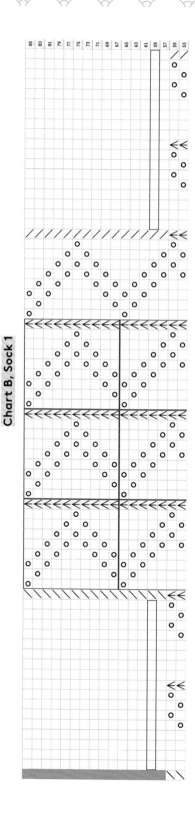

Chart B, Sock 1

Chart A, Sock 2

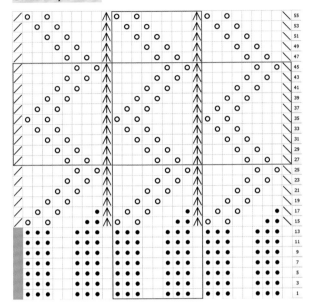

Heel & Toe – Sock 2

Continue from Chart B, Sock 2, beginning with Round 57. Rounds 53/55, which have been worked in the previous chart, are shown here again for orientation—do not work them again.

Work the Heel, starting in Round 59 (framed round) in stockinette stitch, using your preferred method. If working a Round Wedge Heel, follow instructions on page 24.

Continue the stitch pattern on the top of the foot. In Rounds 67 through 86, repeat the stitch pattern on the top of the foot to the beginning of the toe decrease section.

Work the toe decreases in stockinette stitch, using your preferred method as you did for Sock 1.

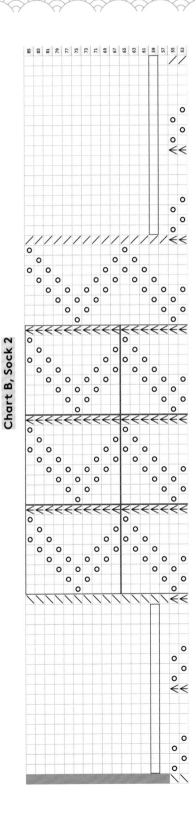

Chart B, Sock 2

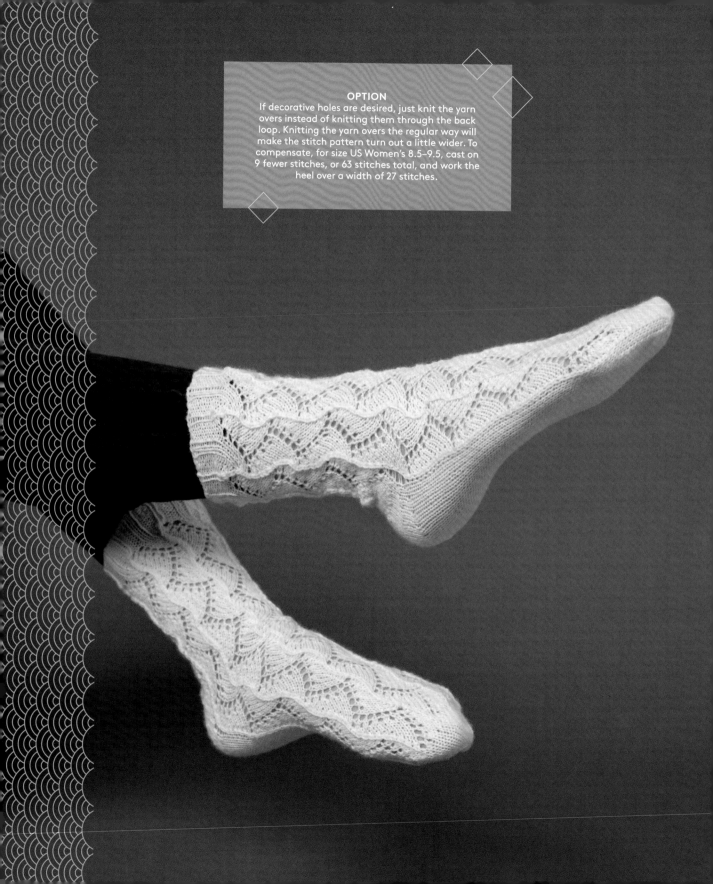

OPTION
If decorative holes are desired, just knit the yarn overs instead of knitting them through the back loop. Knitting the yarn overs the regular way will make the stitch pattern turn out a little wider. To compensate, for size US Women's 8.5–9.5, cast on 9 fewer stitches, or 63 stitches total, and work the heel over a width of 27 stitches.

Suyala Scarf

DIFFICULTY LEVEL

毛糸 毛糸 毛糸

Finished Size

13.8 x 75 in (35 x 190 cm), adjustable

Materials

→ Bunny Light from Filace by Birgit Freyer (50% wool, 25% alpaca, 25% acrylic; 504 yd/460 m per 3.5 oz/100 g); 4 skeins (1.75 oz/ 50 g each) Panna (approx. 875 yd/ 800 m, 6.14 oz/174 g needed)

→ Knitting needles, size US 6 or 7 (4.0 or 4.5 mm)

Gauge Swatch

For this pattern, a gauge swatch is not necessary.

Construction Note

The Scarf is worked from one narrow end to the other. The arrow in the schematic shows the direction of work.

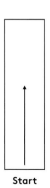

Start

INSTRUCTIONS

Beginning

Cast on 83 stitches. For a narrower/wider scarf, cast on 20 stitches fewer/more.

Continue immediately with Row 1 from Chart A. Only RS rows are shown in the chart. In WS rows, work all stitches as they appear (knit the knits and purl the purls). This means that stitches that had been purled on the RS will now be knitted; all other stitches will be purled. The framed area shows the widthwise pattern repeat; repeat it 4 times across.

Chart A

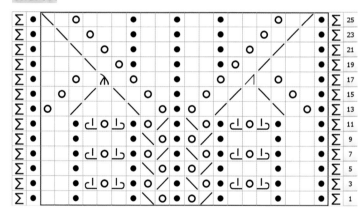

CONTINUED

Middle Part

Continue with Row 27 from Chart B.

Rows 23/25, which have been worked in the previous chart, are shown here again for orientation—do not work them again.

The framed area shows the widthwise pattern repeat; repeat it 4 times across.

Repeat Rows 27 through 56 until a length of approx. 71 in (180 cm) has been reached.

End

Continue with Row 57 from Chart C.

Rows 53/55, which have been worked in the previous chart, are shown here again for orientation—do not work them again.

The framed area shows the widthwise pattern repeat; repeat it 4 times across.

In the last WS row, bind off all stitches, using the elastic bind-off method (see page 14).

Finishing

After the ends have been woven in, soak the Scarf in lukewarm water, press out excess water, and block it to shape.

Chart B

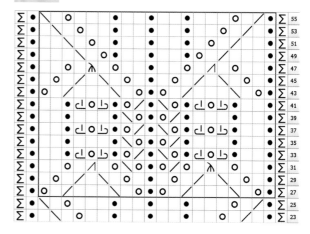

Chart C

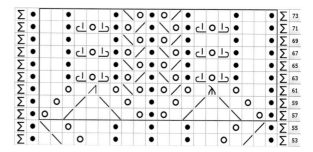

Suyala Poncho

DIFFICULTY LEVEL

毛糸 毛糸 毛糸

Knitting symbol explanations for the charts can be found on page 23.

Finished Size

One size fits most.

Materials

→ Lanartus Alpaca Fine (100% alpaca; 370 yd/338 m per 3.5 oz/ 100 g); 4 skeins (1.75 oz/50 g each) #700 Natural White (approx. 711 yd/650 m, 7 oz/197 g needed)

→ Knitting needles, US size 6 or 7 (4.0 or 4.5 mm)

→ Crochet hook in the same size

Gauge Swatch

For this pattern, a gauge swatch is not necessary.

Construction Note

The Poncho is worked in two Rectangles. Arrows in the schematic show the direction of work. The size of each of the two Rectangles should be approx. 19.7 x 27.5 in (50 x 70 cm). These two Rectangles will be sewn together as described in the Finishing section.

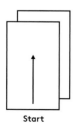

Start

PLEASE NOTE
Work the Poncho from the same knitting charts as Suyala Scarf; see pages 74 and 76.

INSTRUCTIONS

Beginning

Cast on 83 stitches. For a smaller/larger Poncho, cast on 20 stitches fewer/ more.
Continue immediately with Row 1 from Chart A (see page 74). Only RS rows are shown in the chart. In WS rows, work all stitches as they appear (knit the knits and purl the purls). This means that stitches that had been purled on the RS will now be knitted; all other stitches will be purled. The framed area shows the widthwise pattern repeat; repeat it 4 times across.

Middle Part

Continue with Row 27 from Chart B (see page 76).
Rows 23/25, which have been worked in the previous chart, are shown here again for orientation—do not work them again.
The framed area shows the widthwise pattern repeat; repeat it 4 times across.
Repeat Rows 27 through 56 until a length of approx. 23.6 in (60 cm) has been reached.

End

Continue with Row 57 from Chart C (see page 76).
Rows 53/55, which have been worked in the previous chart, are shown here again for orientation—do not work them again.
The framed area shows the widthwise pattern repeat; repeat it 4 times across.
In the last WS row, bind off all stitches, using the elastic bind-off method (see page 14). Work the second Rectangle the same way.

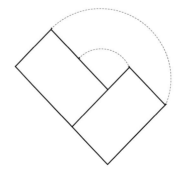

Finishing

Sew the Rectangles together as shown. The dashed lines show how to fold and where to sew together. Finish the neckline by adding a crocheted edging of 1 round single crochet and 1 round reverse single crochet.
After the ends have been woven in, soak the Poncho in lukewarm water, press out excess water, and block it to shape.

Knitting symbol explanations for the charts can be found on page 23.

Suyala Poncho

DIFFICULTY LEVEL

毛糸 毛糸 毛糸

Finished Size

One size fits most.

Materials

→ Kentara from Filace by Birgit Freyer (100% merino wool; 984 yd/900 m per 3.5 oz/100 g); 2 skeins (1.75 oz/50 g each) Beige (approx. 711 yd/650 m, 2.5 oz/ 72 g needed)

→ Knitting needles, US size 6 or 7 (4.0 or 4.5 mm)

→ Crochet hook in the same size

Gauge Swatch

For this pattern, a gauge swatch is not necessary.

Construction Note

For Option 2, a longer Rectangle is knitted. The arrow in the schematic shows the direction of work. This Rectangle is approx. 19.7 x 71 in (50 x 180 cm) and will later be partially seamed as described in the Finishing section.

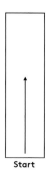

Start

INSTRUCTIONS

Rectangle

Cast on 83 stitches.

Work the beginning as for Option 1. During the Middle Part, repeat Rows 27 through 56 until a length of approx. 67 in (170 cm) has been reached. Work the End the same as for Option 1 again (see page 78).

Finishing

Seam two sections of a side of the Rectangle over a length of about 15.8 in (40 cm). The dashed lines show how to sew the two edges together.

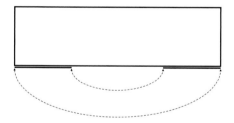

Finish the neckline by adding a crocheted edging of 1 round single crochet and 1 round reverse single crochet.

After the ends have been woven in, soak the Poncho in lukewarm water, press out excess water, and block it to shape.

PLEASE NOTE
Work the Poncho from the same knitting charts as Suyala Scarf; see pages 74 and 76.

Suyala Poncho

DIFFICULTY LEVEL

毛糸 毛糸 毛糸

Knitting symbol explanations for the charts can be found on page 23.

Finished Size

One size fits most.

Materials

→ Bunny Light from Filace by Birgit Freyer (50% wool, 25% alpaca, 25% acrylic; 504 yd/460 m per 3.5 oz/100 g); 4 skeins (1.75 oz/ 50 g each) Panna (approx. 875 yd/800 m, 6.14 oz/174 g needed)

→ Knitting needles, size US 6 or 7 (4.0 to 4.5 mm)

→ Crochet hook in the same size

Gauge Swatch

For this pattern, a gauge swatch is not necessary.

Construction Note

For Option 3, a longer Rectangle is knitted. The arrow in the schematic shows the direction of work. This Rectangle is approx. 23.6 x 51.2 in (60 x 130 cm). The Rectangle is later partially seamed as described in the Finishing section.

Start

INSTRUCTIONS

Rectangle

Cast on 103 stitches.

Work the beginning as for Option 1, but work the widthwise pattern repeat 5 times across. During the Middle Part, repeat Rows 27 through 56 until a length of approx. 47.2 in (120 cm) has been reached. Work the end as for Option 1 again (see page 78).

Finishing

Sew the narrow end of the Rectangle to part of the long side as shown. The dashed lines indicate how to sew the edges together.

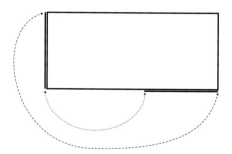

Finish the neckline by adding a crocheted edging of 1 round single crochet and 1 round reverse single crochet. After the ends have been woven in, soak the Poncho in lukewarm water, press out excess water, and block it to shape.

PLEASE NOTE
Work the Poncho from the same knitting charts as Suyala Scarf; see pages 74 and 76.

Hoshiko
Triangular Shawl

DIFFICULTY LEVEL

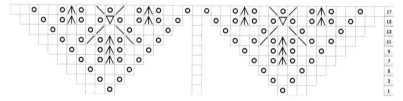

Knitting symbol explanations for the charts can be found on page 23.

Finished Size

33.5 x 75 in (85 x 190 cm), adjustable

Materials

→ Lang Yarns Cashmere Lace (100% cashmere; 722 yd/660 m per 3.5 oz/100 g); 5 skeins (0.88 oz/25 g each) #02 Off White (approx. 820 yd/750 m, 4 oz/114 g needed)

→ Circular knitting needle, US size 6 or 7 (4.0 or 4.5 mm)

→ Crochet hook in the same size

Construction Note

The Shawl is worked from the center out, starting at the long edge at the top—see schematic. The arrows in the schematic show the direction of work.

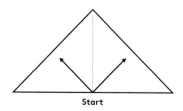

Start

Gauge Swatch

For this pattern, a gauge swatch is not necessary since the main pattern is repeated until the desired size has almost been reached.

INSTRUCTIONS

Beginning

Cast on 5 stitches. In the following WS row, and all other WS rows, purl all stitches. Chart A shows the complete Setup Rows section. Only RS rows are shown in the chart.

Chart A, Setup Rows

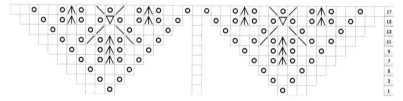

CONTINUED

Main Part (Body of the Shawl)
Continue, working Rows 19 through 34 from Chart B. Row 17, which has been worked earlier, is shown here again for better orientation—do not work it again. The framed area shows the widthwise pattern repeat. First, work the widthwise pattern repeat 2 times for each side.

Work Rows 19 through 34 a total of 8 times. With every subsequent repeat, the widthwise pattern repeat will be worked 2 times more for each side. For a smaller or larger Shawl, one repeat may be omitted or additionally worked.

Transition to Edge
Continue with Rows 35 through 66 from Chart C. Row 33, which has been worked earlier, is shown here again for better orientation—do not work it again.
The framed area shows the widthwise pattern repeat; repeat it across as often as the stitch count permits.

Edge
Continue with Row 67 from Chart D.
Row 65, which has been worked earlier, is shown here again for better orientation—do not work it again. The framed area shows the widthwise pattern repeat. Work the widthwise pattern repeat as often as the stitch count permits.

In Row 81, 3 yarn overs ③ will be worked. In the following WS row, work 3 stitches together into each yarn over as follows: purl 1, knit 1, purl 1. This will, in the last pattern row (Row 83), yield 3 knit stitches in one spot.

> **TIP**
> For a less prominent hole, you may work just 2 instead of 3 yarn overs in the pattern row. However, in the following WS row, still work the same 3 stitches together into each yarn over: purl 1, knit 1, purl 1.

In Row 85, bind off all stitches with a crochet hook, with 1 chain in between (see pages 14 and 15). This sometimes involves crocheting together 3 or 4 stitches according to the number shown in the box.

Finishing
After the ends have been woven in, soak the Shawl in lukewarm water, gently press out excess water, and block it.

Chart B, Main Part (Body of the Shawl)

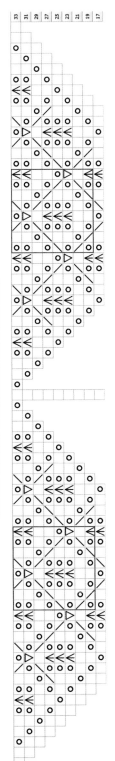

Chart C, Transition to Edge

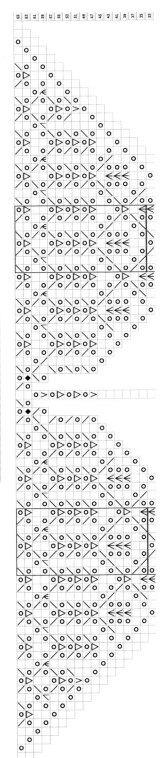

Chart D, Edge

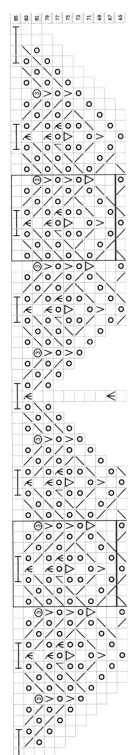

Tomomi Tubular Cowl

Knitting symbol explanations for the charts can be found on page 23.

DIFFICULTY LEVEL

毛糸 毛糸 毛糸

Finished Size

Circumference: 21.7 in (55 cm)
Length: 23.6 in (60 cm)

Materials

→ Lanartus Baby Alpaca Lace (100% alpaca; 874 yd/800 m per 3.5 oz/100 g); 2 skeins (1.75 oz/ 50 g each) #501 Ecru (approx. 601 yd/550 m, 2.4 oz/68 g needed)
→ Circular knitting needle, US size 6 to 8 (4.0 to 5.0 mm)
→ Crochet hook in the same size

Construction Note

The Tubular Cowl is worked in one piece in the round and can be worn as a head covering or a neck warmer.

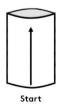

Start

Gauge Swatch

Work the gauge swatch in back-and-forth rows with turning. Cast on 26 stitches, and work from Gauge Swatch Chart. Only RS rows are shown in the chart. In WS rows, purl all stitches and yarn overs. After Row 32, bind off all stitches loosely.

Wash the gauge swatch, and let it dry spread out flat. When dry, measure the width of the swatch. The section from stitch #13 through stitch #24 (denoted by arrows under the chart) should measure 2 in (5 cm) in width.

Gauge Swatch Chart

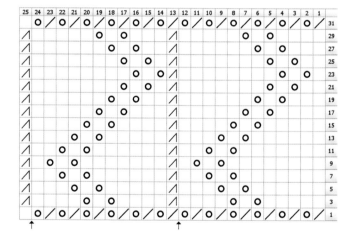

IF THE WIDTH DOES NOT MATCH OR A DIFFERENT WIDTH IS NEEDED
Adjust by using a smaller or larger needle size. However, if you like the stitch definition the original needle size gives and would like to keep it, you need to calculate a different stitch count.

EXAMPLE
The circumference should be approx. 23.6 in (60 cm).
Your gauge swatch from stitch #13 through #24 had 2.2 in (5.5 cm).
23.6 in (60 cm) / 2.2 in (5.5 cm) = 10.7 (10.9), rounded up to 11
11 x 2.2 in (5.5 cm) = 24.2 in (60.5 cm)
One widthwise pattern repeat will have 12 stitches.
11 x 12 stitches = 132 stitches

INSTRUCTIONS

Beginning

Cast on 144 stitches, and join in the round. Continue from Tubular Cowl Chart.

In every other round, knit all stitches.

Stitch Pattern

Work from Tubular Cowl Chart.

In the chart, 12 stitches are shown; repeat these as often as the stitch count permits.

The framed area (Rounds 3 through 30) shows the heightwise pattern repeat; repeat it to the desired length.

In Round 35, bind off all stitches loosely.

Finishing

Finish the Tubular Cowl by adding a round of crocheted picots at both ends. For this, work "1 single crochet, chain 3, and again 1 single crochet" into each yarn over from Rounds 1 and 33.

After the ends have been woven in, soak the Tubular Cowl in lukewarm water, gently press out excess water, and pull it into the finished shape.

Tubular Cowl Chart

1	2	3	4	5	6	7	8	9	10	11	12	Round
O	/	O	/	O	/	O	/	O	/	O	/	33
⟋	O		O									31
⟋		O		O								29
⟋			O		O							27
⟋				O		O						25
⟋					O		O					23
⟋						O		O				21
⟋							O		O			19
⟋								O		O	O	17
⟋								O		O		15
⟋							O		O			13
⟋						O		O				11
⟋					O		O					9
⟋				O		O						7
⟋			O		O							5
⟋		O		O								3
O	/	O	/	O	/	O	/	O	/	O	/	1

Kisaki Cardigan

Knitting symbol explanations for the charts can be found on page 23.

DIFFICULTY LEVEL

毛糸 毛糸 毛糸

Finished Size

Adjustable

Materials

→ Lanartus Fine Merino Socks (75% merino wool fine, superwash, 25% polyamide; 459 yd/420 m per 3.5 oz/100 g); in #100 White, total depends on finished size: approx. 1,203 yd (1,100 m), 10.6 oz (300 g) for a long-sleeve cardigan 23.6 in (60 cm) long in size US 8; 1,640 yd (1,500 m), 14.1 oz (400 g) for a long-sleeve cardigan 23.6 in (60 cm) long in size US 10 (yarn comes in 3.5 oz/100 g skeins; you will need 3 [4] skeins for sizes above; estimate as needed for other sizes)

→ Circular knitting needle, US size 6 or 7 (4.0 or 4.5 mm)

→ Crochet hook in the same size

Gauge Swatch

For this pattern, a gauge swatch is not necessary since increases are worked until the desired size has been reached.

Construction Note

The cardigan is worked in top-down raglan construction. All stitches (Front – Sleeve – Back – Sleeve – Front) are cast on and worked together in one piece. The arrows in the schematic show the direction of work.

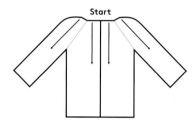

At the transitions between Sleeves and Body, in every other round, 2 stitches each are increased, meaning every other round will have 8 stitches more. The increases are accounted for in the chart.

INSTRUCTIONS

Beginning

Cast on 111 stitches. The number |1| indicates the raglan line stitch.

27 Front	|1| |1|	11 Sleeve	|1| |1|	31 Back	|1| |1|	11 Sleeve	|1| |1|	27 Front

In the following WS row, purl all stitches.
Continue from Chart A, first working Rows 1 through 10. Only RS rows are shown in the chart. In WS rows, almost all stitches are purled. For ⌐~⌐, knit stitches are worked on the WS.
The widthwise pattern repeat is framed in bold. Due to space constraints, the Sleeves and the Back are not shown here separately.

Chart A

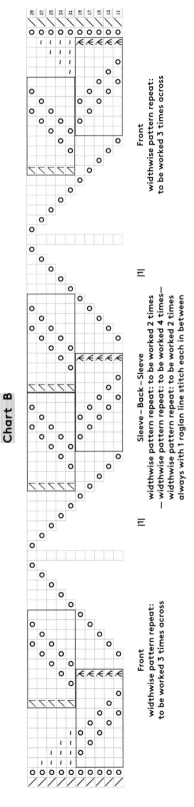

27 Lace Front
widthwise pattern repeat:
to be worked 2 times across

|1|

11 Lace Sleeve – 31 Lace Back – 11 Lace Sleeve
widthwise pattern repeat: to be worked 1 time –
widthwise pattern repeat: to be worked 3 times
– widthwise pattern repeat: to be worked 1 time
always with 1 raglan line stitch each in between

|1|

27 Lace Front
widthwise pattern repeat:
to be worked 2 times across

Continue with Row 11 from Chart B.

Chart B

Front
widthwise pattern repeat:
to be worked 3 times across

|1|

Sleeve – Back – Sleeve
widthwise pattern repeat: to be worked 2 times
– widthwise pattern repeat: to be worked 4 times–
widthwise pattern repeat: to be worked 2 times
always with 1 raglan line stitch each in between

|1|

Front
widthwise pattern repeat:
to be worked 3 times across

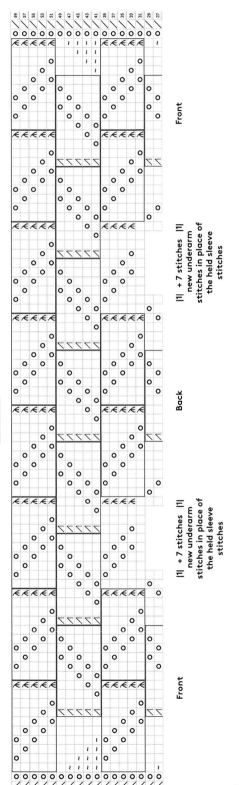

Chart C

Front

|I| +7 stitches |I|
new underarm
stitches in place of
the held sleeve
stitches

Back

|I| +7 stitches |I|
new underarm
stitches in place of
the held sleeve
stitches

Front

Repeat Rows 11 through 30 (= 1 heightwise pattern repeat) until the desired width for the chest circumference has almost been reached. With every subsequent repeat, the stitch count and, with it, the number of widthwise pattern repeats, will increase.

NOTE ABOUT LARGER SIZES
The raglan line (the 1 stitch between Body and Sleeves) for size US 12/14 should be approx. 10.6 in (27 cm) long. For larger sizes, this line will automatically become longer. However, the raglan line should not turn out too long, which would result in a too wide (and, therefore, too deep) armhole. If this is the case, a larger number of stitches (1 widthwise pattern repeat = 10 stitches more) will be cast on using the backward-loop cast-on method. More about this in the next section.

Main Part (Body)
In Row 31, the sleeve stitches are transferred to a stitch holder or piece of waste yarn for holding and not worked at this time. The raglan line stitches are added to the Body sections.

PLEASE NOTE
I recommend using a thick piece of yarn in a contrasting color for holding the sleeve stitches.

In place of the now-held sleeve stitches, cast on 7 new underarm stitches between Front and Back as well as Back and Front by using the backward-loop cast-on method.

IF WORKING LARGER SIZES
Instead of 7 new underarm stitches, 17 stitches can be cast on using the backward-loop cast-on method, to prevent the raglan line from becoming too long. In this case, the widthwise pattern repeat (10 stitches wide) will be repeated more often.

Continue, working Front, Back, and Front together in one piece.
Continue from Chart C, beginning with Row 31.
The framed area shows the widthwise pattern repeat; repeat it across as often as the stitch count permits. Rows 27/29, which have been worked earlier, are shown here again for better orientation—do not work them again here. Repeat Rows 41 through 60 until the desired length, minus approx. 2 in (5 cm) for the final rows, has been reached.

CONTINUED

Final Rows

Continue from Chart D, working Rows 61 through 70. Rows 57/59, which have been worked in the previous chart, are shown here again for orientation. The framed area shows the widthwise pattern repeat (10 stitches wide); repeat it across as often as the stitch count permits.

PLEASE NOTE

For ■, knit stitches will be worked on the WS. In the last WS row (Row 70), all stitches will be knit. After Row 70, all stitches will be bound off.

Chart D

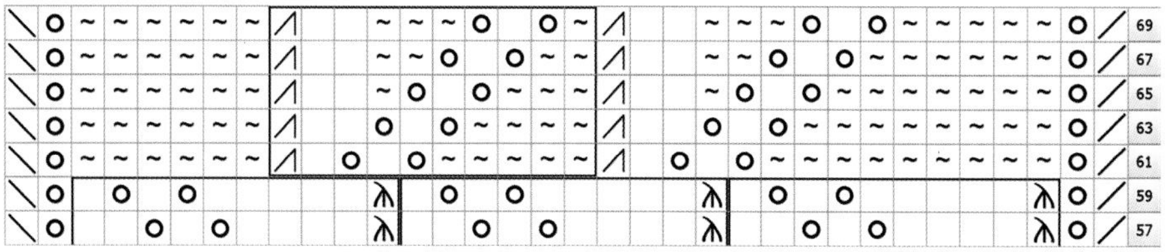

Sleeves

The Sleeves are worked in the round; in even-numbered rounds, all stitches are knitted. Take up the previously held sleeve stitches, and place them on the needle. Additionally, work 9 stitches into the corresponding cast-on underarm stitches. (Please note for larger sizes: If at the Body, 17 stitches had been previously cast on between Front and Back/Back and Front, you will now work 19 stitches into the corresponding cast-on un-derarm stitches.) The beginning of the round is exactly in the middle of the additionally cast-on underarm stitches. Work the stitch pattern over all stitches, includ-ing the sleeve stitches. Continue from Chart E, Round 31: work 5 stitches into the corresponding underarm stitches, work over the formerly held sleeve stitches, work 4 stitches into the corresponding cast-on underarm stitches.

Rows 27/29, which have been worked earlier, are shown here again for orientation—do not work them again.

Chart E

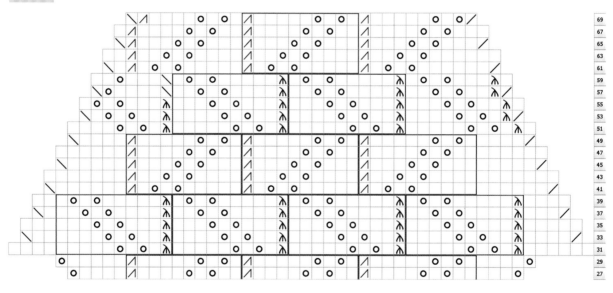

In every 5th round, at the beginning and the end of the round, knit 2 stitches together each, until the stitch count is a multiple of 10, such as, for instance, 50 stitches.

Continue from Chart F, Round 71.

Repeat Rounds 81 through 100 until the desired sleeve length, minus approx. 2 in (5 cm) for the final rounds, has been reached. Finally, work Rounds 101 through 109. In the last round (Round 110), purl all stitches.

After having completed Round 110, bind off all stitches.

Chart F

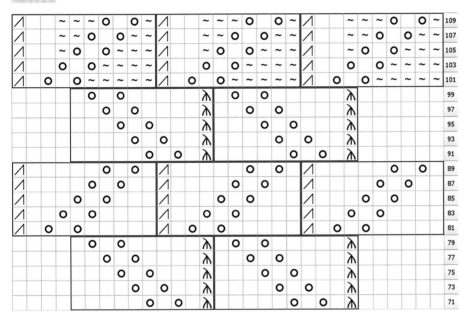

Finishing

Finish the neckline and front edges by adding a crocheted edging of 1 row single crochet and 1 row reverse
single crochet. If buttonholes will be added, work
chains instead of single crochets in the appropriate
spots during the first edging row, and work the reverse
single crochet in the chain space in the following row.
After the ends have been woven in, soak the Cardigan
in lukewarm water, gently press out excess water, and
block to shape.

Kisaki Pullover

Knitting symbol explanations for the charts can be found on page 23.

DIFFICULTY LEVEL

毛糸 毛糸 毛糸

Finished Size

Adjustable

Materials

→ BabyCotton from Filace by Birgit Freyer (100% cotton; 394 yd/360 m per 3.5 oz/100 g); in Onice, total depends on finished size: approx. 930 yd (850 m), 8.3 oz (236 g) for a long-sleeve sweater in size US 6/8; 1,312 yd (1,200 m), 11.8 oz (333 g) for a long-sleeve sweater in size US 12/14 (yarn comes in 1.75 oz/50 g skeins; you will need 5 [7] skeins for sizes above; estimate as needed for other sizes)

→ Circular knitting needle, US size 6 or 7 (4.0 or 4.5 mm)

→ Crochet hook in the same size

Gauge Swatch

For this pattern, a gauge swatch is not necessary since increases are worked until the desired size has been reached.

Construction Note

The sweater is worked in top-down raglan construction. All stitches (Front – Sleeve – Back – Sleeve) are cast on and worked together in one piece. The arrows in the schematic show the direction of work.

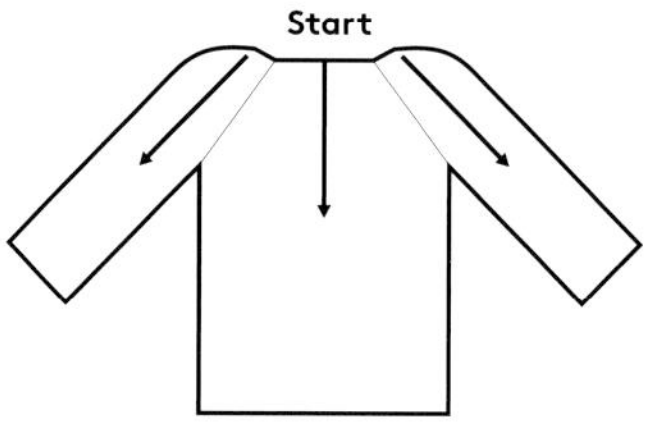

At the transitions between Sleeves and Body, in every other round, 2 stitches each are increased, meaning every other round will have 8 stitches more. The increases are accounted for in the chart.

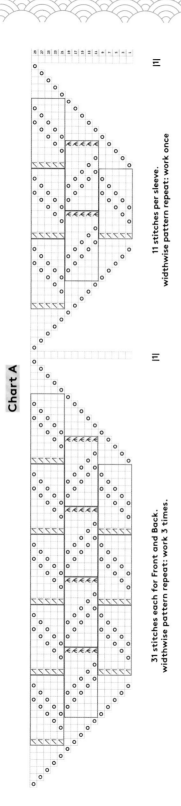

Chart A

11 stitches per sleeve.
widthwise pattern repeat: work once

|1|

|1|

31 stitches each for Front and Back.
widthwise pattern repeat: work 3 times.

INSTRUCTIONS

Beginning
Cast on 88 stitches. The number |1| indicates the raglan line stitch.

31		1		11		1		31		1		11		1	
Front	|1|	Sleeve	|1|	Back	|1|	Sleeve	|1|

Join in the round, and then knit for one round. After this, continue from Chart A. Only pattern rounds are shown in the chart. In even-numbered rounds, knit all stitches. The framed area shows the widthwise pattern repeat. Due to space constraints, only one Sleeve is shown, and the Body is shown only once, but the charts need to be worked twice.

Repeat Rounds 11 through 30 (= 1 heightwise pattern repeat) until the desired width for the chest circumference has almost been reached.
With every subsequent repeat, the stitch count and (with it) the number of widthwise pattern repeats will increase.

> **IMPORTANT**
> It is strongly recommended to mark each raglan line stitch with a stitch marker.
>
> **NOTE ABOUT LARGER SIZES**
> The raglan line (the 1 stitch between Body and Sleeves) for size US 12/14 should be approx. 10.6 in (27 cm) long. For larger sizes, this line will automatically become longer. However, the raglan line should not turn out too long, which would result in a too wide (and, therefore, too deep) armhole. If this is the case, a larger number of stitches (1 widthwise pattern repeat = 10 stitches more) will be cast on using the backward-loop cast-on method. More about this in the next section.

CONTINUED

Main Part (Body)

In Round 30, the sleeve stitches are transferred to a stitch holder or piece of waste yarn for holding and not worked at this time. The raglan line stitches are added to the Body sections.

> **PLEASE NOTE**
> I recommend using a thick piece of yarn in a contrasting color for holding the sleeve stitches.

In place of the now-held sleeve stitches, cast on 7 new underarm stitches between Front and Back as well as Back and Front by using the backward-loop cast-on method. Continue Front, Back, and Front together in one piece.

> **PLEASE NOTE**
> For larger sizes, 17 stitches instead of 7 can be cast on using the backward-loop cast-on method, to prevent the raglan line from becoming too long. In this case, the widthwise pattern repeat (10 stitches wide) will be repeated more often.

Continue from Chart B, beginning with Round 31. The framed area shows the widthwise pattern repeat; repeat it around as often as the stitch count permits. Rounds 27/29, which have been worked earlier, are shown here again for better orientation—do not work them again here.

Continue from Chart C, beginning with Round 41. The framed area shows the widthwise pattern repeat; repeat it around as often as the stitch count permits. Rounds 37/39, which have been worked earlier, are shown here again for better orientation—do not work them again here.

Please note: Every 10 rounds, the beginning of the round moves by a few stitches.

From Round 41 on, the stitch pattern will begin earlier, and from Round 51 on, the stitch pattern will begin later.

Chart B

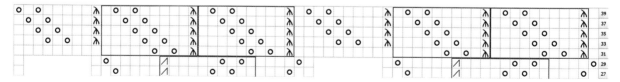

| |1| | + 7 new underarm stitches in place of the held sleeve stitches | |1| | Front | |1| | + 7 new underarm stitches in place of the held sleeve stitches | |1| | Back |

Repeat Rounds 41 through 60 until the desired length, minus approx. 2 in (5 cm) for the final rounds, has been reached. Finally, work Rounds 61 through 70.

PLEASE NOTE
For ■, purl stitches will be worked in even-numbered rounds.

After Row 70, bind off all stitches.

Sleeves

Work the Sleeves for the pullover in the same way as for the Kisaki Cardigan (see pages 100 and 101).

Finishing

Finish the neckline by adding a crocheted edging of 1 round single crochet and 1 round reverse single crochet.
After the ends have been woven in, soak the Pullover in lukewarm water, gently press out excess water, and block to shape.

Chart C

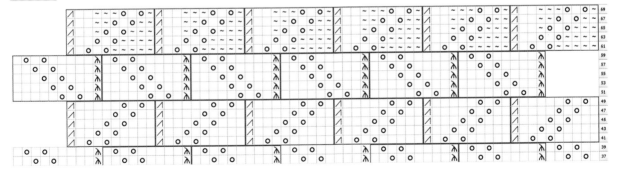

Natsuki Corner Shawl

Knitting symbol explanations for the charts can be found on page 23.

DIFFICULTY LEVEL

毛糸 毛糸 毛糸

Finished Size

27.5 x 78.7 in (70 x 200 cm)

Materials

→ Filace Cleopatra (90% cotton, 10% cashmere; 1,640 yd/1,500 m per 3.5 oz/100 g); 2 skeins (1.75 oz/ 50 g each) Latte (approx. 1,203 yd/1,100 m, 2.6 oz/73 g needed)

→ Circular knitting needle, US size 4 to 7 (3.5 to 4.5 mm)

→ Crochet hook in the same size

Gauge Swatch

For this pattern, a gauge swatch is not necessary.

Construction Note

The Shawl is worked from the interior corner out; see schematic. The arrows in the schematic show the direction of work. The edging is added separately at the end. In different sections, the yarn is held either single or double.

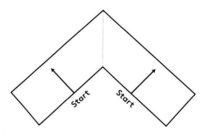

INSTRUCTIONS

Beginning

With 2 strands of yarn held together, cast on 215 stitches. For a shorter/ longer shawl, fewer/more stitches can be cast on in increments of 24. In the following WS row, and all other WS rows, purl all stitches. Continue with Row 1 from Chart A (only RS rows are shown in the chart). These rows are worked with 2 strands of yarn held together. The framed area is the respective widthwise pattern repeat; work it 8 times for each half of the Shawl.

Chart A

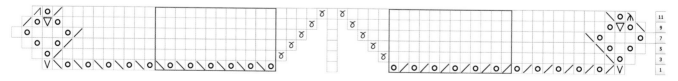

CONTINUED →

After this, continue with Row 13 from Chart B.
Rows 9/11, which have been worked in the previous
chart, are shown here again for orientation—do not
work them again.
Work Rows 13 through 24 with yarn held single.
Work Rows 25 through 36 with yarn held double.
Rows 13 through 36 are the heightwise pattern repeat;
work it 5 times (alternating between yarn held single
and double).

Pointed Edging

Continue with Row 133 from Chart C1. Rows 129/131,
which have already been worked, are shown here
again for orientation. The Pointed Edging is worked
with yarn held single.
The framed area shows the widthwise pattern repeat
for each half of the Shawl; work it as often as the
stitch count for the respective half of the Shawl permits. In Row 143, the lace pattern insert begins. Use
the symbol $\boxed{V}$ for orientation = 2 stitches from 1.
The smaller chart C2 will be inserted into the main
chart in the gray triangular areas (see also page 22).
In Row 153, bind off all stitches with either 1 or 3
chains in between (see pages 14 and 15). This sometimes involves crocheting off 3 or 4 stitches together,
according to the number shown in the box $\boxed{\vdash—\dashv}$. For
$\boxed{\because}$, a chain of 3 is additionally worked between the
bind-off stitches.

Chart C2

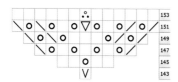

Finishing

After the ends have been woven in, soak the Shawl
in lukewarm water, press out excess water, and block
to shape.

TIP
For the narrower option, Rows 13 through 36 (heightwise pattern repeat) are worked 3 times only.

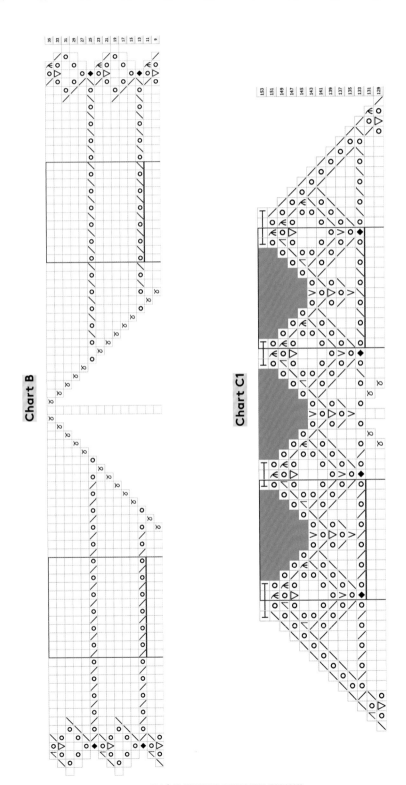

Chart B

Chart C1

Sayuri Arm Warmers

Knitting symbol explanations for the charts can be found on page 23.

DIFFICULTY LEVEL

毛糸 毛糸 毛糸

Finished Size

Circumference: 6.9 in (17.5 cm), adjustable
Length: 8.7 in (22 cm)

Materials

→ KidSeta Lace by Filace by Birgit Freyer (70% mohair, 30% silk; 924 yd/844 m per 3.5 oz/100 g); 1 skein (0.88 oz/25 g) Ecru (approx. 109 yd/100 m, 0.42 oz/12 g needed)
→ Double-pointed needle set, US size 2 to 4 (2.75 to 3.5 mm)

Construction Note

The Arm Warmers are worked in one piece in the round.

Gauge Swatch

Work the gauge swatch in back-and-forth rows with turning. Cast on 19 stitches, and then continue from Gauge Swatch Chart. Only RS rows are shown in the chart. In WS rows, work all stitches as they appear (knit the knits and purl the purls), and purl the yarn overs. After Row 30, bind off all stitches loosely. Wash the gauge swatch, and let it dry spread out flat. When dry, measure the width of the swatch. The section from stitch #3 through stitch #10 (denoted by arrows under the chart) should measure 1.4 in (3.5 cm) in width.

Gauge Swatch Chart

19	18	17	16	15	14	13	12	11	10	9	8	7	6	5	4	3	2	1	
●		O		O			O	Λ	●		O		O		O	Λ	●		29
●		O		O			O	Λ	●		O		O		O	Λ	●		27
●		O		O			O	Λ	●		O		O		O	Λ	●		25
●		O		O			O	Λ	●		O		O		O	Λ	●		23
●		O		O			O	Λ	●		O		O		O	Λ	●		21
●	⅄	O		O		O			●	⅄	O		O		O		●		19
●	⅄	O		O		O			●	⅄	O		O		O		●		17
●	⅄	O		O		O			●	⅄	O		O		O		●		15
●	⅄	O		O		O			●	⅄	O		O		O		●		13
●	⅄	O		O		O			●	⅄	O		O		O		●		11
●		O		O			O	Λ	●		O		O		O	Λ	●		9
●		O		O			O	Λ	●		O		O		O	Λ	●		7
●		O		O			O	Λ	●		O		O		O	Λ	●		5
●		O		O			O	Λ	●		O		O		O	Λ	●		3
●		O		O			O	Λ	●		O		O		O	Λ	●		1

IF THE WIDTH DOES NOT MATCH OR A DIFFERENT WIDTH IS NEEDED
Adjust by using a smaller or larger needle size. However, if you like the stitch definition the original needle size gives and would like to keep it, you need to calculate a different stitch count.

EXAMPLE
The circumference should be approx. 6.7 to 7.1 in (17 to 18 cm).
Your gauge swatch from stitch #3 through #10 measures 1.2 in (3 cm).
6.7 in (17 cm) / 1.2 in (3 cm) = 5.6, rounded up to 6
6 x 1.2 in (3 cm) = 7.2 in (18 cm)
One widthwise pattern repeat will have 8 stitches.
6 x 8 stitches = 48 stitches

INSTRUCTIONS

Casting On and Working the Stitch Pattern

Cast on 40 stitches, and join in the round. Continue from Arm Warmer Chart. Only pattern rounds are shown in the chart. In even-numbered rounds, work all stitches as they appear (knit the knits, and purl the purls), and knit the yarn overs. In the chart, the widthwise pattern repeat is 8 stitches wide; repeat it as often around as the stitch count permits. First, work Rounds 1 through 12 once. The framed area (Rounds 13 through 32) shows the heightwise pattern repeat; repeat it to the desired length. After this, work Rounds 33 through 41 once. In Round 42, bind off all stitches, using the elastic bind-off method (see page 14).

Arm Warmer Chart

~	~	~	~	~	~	~		41
~	~	~	~	~	~	~		39
~	~	~	~	~	~	~		37
~	~	~	~	~	~	~		35
~	~	~	~	~	~	~		33
⋏	O		O		O		●	31
⋏	O		O		O		●	29
⋏	O		O		O		●	27
⋏	O		O		O		●	25
⋏	O		O		O		●	23
	O		O		O	⋏	●	21
	O		O		O	⋏	●	19
	O		O		O	⋏	●	17
	O		O		O	⋏	●	15
	O		O		O	⋏	●	13
●		●		●		●		11
●		●		●		●		9
●		●		●		●		7
●		●		●		●		5
●		●		●		●		3
●		●		●		●		1

Finishing

After the ends have been woven in, soak the Arm Warmers in lukewarm water, press out excess water, and block to shape.

Hanayo Cowl

DIFFICULTY LEVEL

毛糸 毛糸 毛糸

Knitting symbol
explanations
for the charts
can be found
on page 23.

Finished Size

Circumference: 19.7 in (50 cm)
Width: 10 in (25 cm)

Materials

→ Bunny Light from Filace by Birgit
Freyer (50% wool, 25% alpaca,
25% acrylic; 504 yd/460 m per
3.5 oz/100 g); 1 skein (1.75 oz/50
g) Panna (approx. 164 yd/150 m,
1.2 oz/33 g needed)

→ Circular knitting needle, US size 6
or 7 (4.0 or 4.5 mm)

Construction Note

The Cowl is worked as a tube in the
round. The arrow in the schematic
shows the direction of work.

Start

Gauge Swatch

Work the gauge swatch in back-and-forth rows with turning. Cast on 27
stitches, and then continue from Gauge Swatch Chart. Only RS rows are
shown in the chart. In WS rows, work all stitches as they appear (knit the
knits and purl the purls), and purl the yarn overs. After Row 24, bind off
all stitches loosely.

Wash the gauge swatch, and let it dry spread out flat. When dry, measure
the width of the swatch. The section from stitch #2 through stitch #25 (denoted by arrows under the chart) should measure 4.33 in (11 cm) in width.

Gauge Swatch Chart

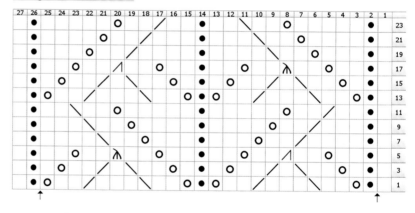

IF THE WIDTH DOES NOT MATCH OR A DIFFERENT WIDTH IS NEEDED
Adjust by using a smaller or larger needle size. However, if you like the
stitch definition the original needle size gives and would like to keep it,
you need to calculate a different stitch count.

EXAMPLE
Your circumference should be approx. 21.7 in (55 cm).
Your gauge swatch from stitch #2 to #25 measures 3.5 in (9 cm).
21.7 in (55 cm) / 3.5 in (9 cm) = 6.2, rounded down: 6
6 x 3.5 in (9 cm) = 21 in (54 cm)
One widthwise pattern repeat will have 24 stitches.
6 x 24 stitches = 144 stitches

INSTRUCTIONS

Casting On and Working the Stitch Pattern

The Cowl is worked in the round. Cast on 120 stitches (= approx. 21.7 in/55 cm), and join in the round. For a cowl with a smaller/larger circumference, fewer/more stitches may be cast on in increments of 24.

Continue from Cowl Chart. Only pattern rounds are shown in the chart.

In even-numbered rounds, work all stitches as they appear (knit the knits, and purl the purls), and knit the yarn overs. The wide framed area shows the widthwise pattern repeat (24 stitches); repeat it around as often as the stitch count permits.

The tall, framed area (Rounds 17 through 40) shows the heightwise pattern repeat. Repeat the heightwise pattern more often if a taller cowl is desired.

Now work the final Rounds 41 through 60.

After this, bind off all stitches, using the elastic bind-off method (see page 14).

Cowl Chart

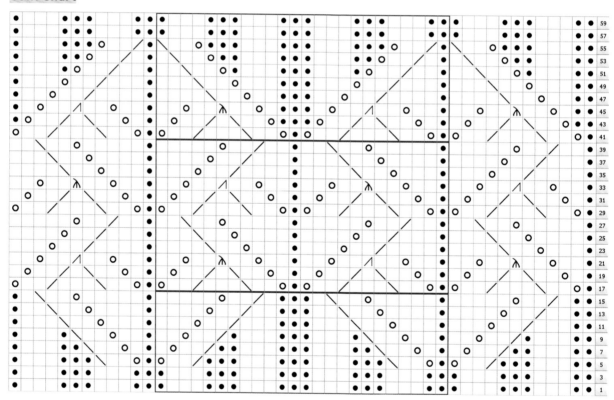

Finishing

After the ends have been woven in, soak the Cowl in lukewarm water, gently press out excess water, and pull it into the finished shape.

Ayumi Stole

DIFFICULTY LEVEL

毛糸 毛糸 毛糸

Finished Size

29.5 x 71 in (75 x 180 cm), adjustable

Materials

→ Schoppel Twister Lace (75% merino wool fine superwash, 25% silk; 656 yd/600 m per 3.5 oz/100 g); 2 skeins (3.5 oz/100 g each) #980 Nature (approx. 1,312 yd/1,200 m, 7 oz/200 g needed)

→ Circular knitting needle, US size 6 to 8 (4.0 to 5.0 mm)

→ Crochet hook in the same size

Gauge Swatch

For this pattern, a gauge swatch is not necessary since the main pattern is repeated until the desired size has almost been reached.

Construction Note

The Stole is worked in one piece. The arrow in the schematic shows the direction of work.

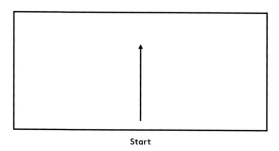

Start

INSTRUCTIONS

Beginning & Main Part (Body of the Stole)

Loosely cast on 309 stitches. If a stole shorter/longer than 71 in (180 cm) is desired, cast on fewer/more stitches in increments of 28.
In the next WS row and all following WS rows, purl all stitches. Continue from Chart A. Only RS rows are shown in the chart. The framed area (28 stitches) shows the widthwise pattern repeat; repeat it 10 times across.

Chart A

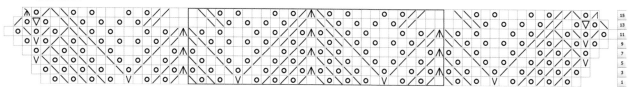

CONTINUED

After this, continue with Row 17 from Chart B. Row 15, which has been worked earlier, is shown here again for better orientation—do not work it again. The framed area (28 stitches) shows the widthwise pattern repeat; repeat it 10 times across.

Work Rows 17 through 24 a total of 13 times. For a scarf, work Rows 17 through 24 a total of 6 times only (see page 124).

Chart B

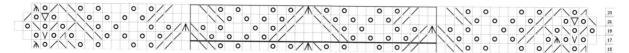

Edging

Work the Edging from Chart C, beginning with Row 25. Row 23, which has been worked earlier, is shown here again for better orientation—do not work it again. The framed area (28 stitches) shows the widthwise pattern repeat; repeat it 10 times across.

In Row 43, bind off all stitches with either 1 or 3 chains in between (see pages 14 and 15). This sometimes involves crocheting 3 stitches ⊢——⊣ off together. For ⦂, a chain of 3 is additionally worked between the bind-off stitches.

Chart C

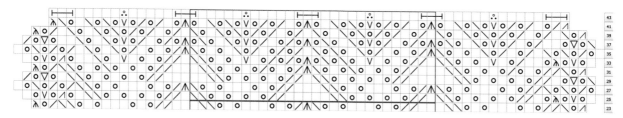

Finishing

After the ends have been woven in, soak the Stole in lukewarm water, press out excess water, and block to shape.

Ayumi Scarf

Finished Size

16 x 71 in (40 x 180 cm), adjustable

Materials

→ Coast Lacegarn from Filace by
  Birgit Freyer (55% wool, 45%
  cotton; 764 yd/698 m per 3.5
  oz/100 g); 2 skeins (1.75 oz/50
  g each) Ecru (approx. 711
  yd/650 m, 3.3 oz/93 g needed)

→ Circular knitting needle, US size
  6 to 8 (4.0 to 5.0 mm)

→ Crochet hook in the same size

Gauge Swatch

For this pattern, a gauge swatch is
not necessary since the main pattern is repeated until the desired
size has almost been reached.

Construction Note

The Scarf is worked in one piece (see Ayumi Stole, page 120).

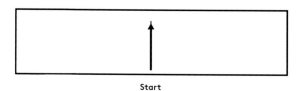

Start

INSTRUCTIONS

The Scarf is worked from the same instructions as the Ayumi Stole.
Rows 17 through 24 are worked a total of 6 times.

Akira Socks

DIFFICULTY LEVEL

毛糸 毛糸 毛糸

Knitting symbol explanations for the charts can be found on page 23.

Finished Size

US Women's 7.5 to 9.5, adjustable

Materials

→ Schoppel Admiral (75% pure new wool, superwash, 25% pol-yamide; 459 yd/420 m per 3.5 oz/100 g); 1 skein (3.5 oz/100 g) #980 Nature (approx. 328 yd/ 300 m, 2.5 oz/71 g needed)
→ Double-pointed needle set, US size 1 (2.0 to 2.25 mm)

Construction Note

The Socks are worked in the round from the cuff down to the toe.

Gauge Swatch

For this pattern, a gauge swatch is not necessary.

INSTRUCTIONS

Cast On & Leg

Cast on 68 stitches, and join in the round.

Continue from Chart A. Only pattern rounds are shown in the chart. In even-numbered rounds, work all stitches as they appear (knit the knits, and purl the purls). Knit the yarn overs through the back loop (twisted). The chart shows one widthwise pattern repeat (17 stitches); work it 4 times around.

The framed area (Rounds 31–42) shows the heightwise pattern repeat. Repeat the heightwise pattern repeat until the leg is approx. 1.2 in (3 cm) shorter than the desired length.

Chart A

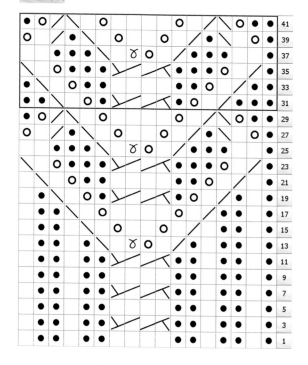

CONTINUED   →

Heel & Toe

Continue from Chart B, starting with Round 43.
Round 41, which has been worked earlier, is shown here
again for better orientation—do not work it again.
Work the Heel, starting in Round 61, in stockinette
stitch, using your preferred method. If working a
Round Wedge Heel, follow instructions on page 24.

Continue the stitch pattern on the top of the foot.
Repeat the pattern in Rounds 55 through 66 on the
top of the foot to the beginning of the toe decreases,
approx. 1.2 in (3 cm) before the desired length. Finally,
work Rounds 67 through 82 once.
Work the toe decreases in stockinette stitch, using
your preferred method. A technique tutorial for toe
decreases is included on page 25.

Chart B

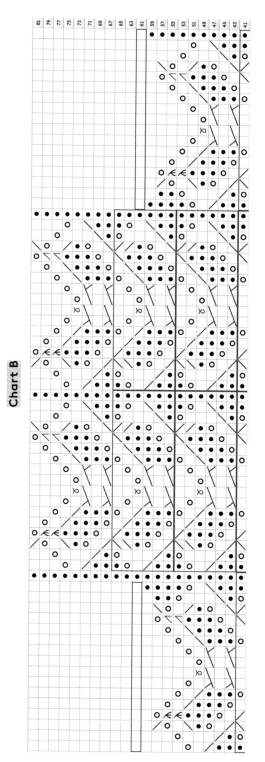

Umeko Stole

DIFFICULTY LEVEL

毛糸 毛糸 毛糸

Finished Size

39.4 x 78.7 in (100 x 200 cm)

Materials

→ Filace Setamo (50% silk, 50% mohair; 1,640 yd/1,500 m per 3.5 oz/100 g); 4 skeins (0.88 oz/ 25 g each) Ecru (approx. 1,640 yd/1,500 m, 3.5 oz/100 g needed)

→ Circular knitting needle, US size 6 or 7 (4.0 or 4.5 mm)

Gauge Swatch

For this pattern, a gauge swatch is not necessary.

Construction Note

The Stole is worked in one piece. The arrow in the schematic shows the direction of work.

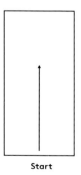

Start

INSTRUCTIONS

Cast on 145 stitches. In the next WS row and all following WS rows, purl all stitches. Continue from Stole Chart. Only RS rows are shown in the chart. Rows 45 through 96 are the heightwise pattern repeat. Work the height-wise pattern repeat 9 times in all. For a shorter/longer stole, the height-wise pattern repeat can be worked fewer/more times. Afterward, finish by working Rows 97 through 140. After having completed the last WS row, bind off all stitches loosely.

> **PLEASE NOTE**
> The chart for this pattern is included as a fold-out.

Finishing

After the ends have been woven in, wash the Stole in lukewarm water, gently press out excess water, and block it.

Kiyoe Scarf

DIFFICULTY LEVEL

毛糸 毛糸 毛糸

Knitting symbol explanations for the charts can be found on page 23.

Finished Size

16 x 71 in (40 x 180 cm), adjustable

Materials

→ Lang Yarns Lusso (36% merino wool, 27% silk, 19% camel hair, 18% mohair; 787.4 yd/720 m per 3.5 oz/100 g); 3 skeins (0.88 oz/ 25 g each) #03 Light Gray Heathered (approx. 580 yd/ 530 m, 2.6 oz/74 g needed, depending on finished size)

→ Knitting needles, US size 6 to 8 (4.0 to 5.0 mm)

Gauge Swatch

For this pattern, a gauge swatch is not necessary.

Construction Note

The Scarf is worked from one narrow end to the other. The arrow in the schematic shows the direction of work.

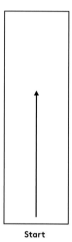

Start

INSTRUCTIONS

Cast On
Cast on 76 stitches. Continue directly with Row 1 from the Scarf Chart.

Stitch Pattern
First, work Rows 1 through 12 once. Only RS rows are shown in the chart. In the first 3 WS rows, knit all stitches.
The framed area shows the widthwise pattern repeat; work it 2 times. From Rows 8 through 30, purl all stitches in WS rows.

The framed area (Rows 13 to 24) shows the heightwise pattern repeat, which is repeated until the desired length has almost been reached. Finish by working Rows 25 through 36.
In the last 3 WS rows, knit all stitches. Finally, bind off all stitches loosely.

Finishing
After the ends have been woven in, soak the Scarf in lukewarm water, press out excess water, and block it.

Scarf Chart

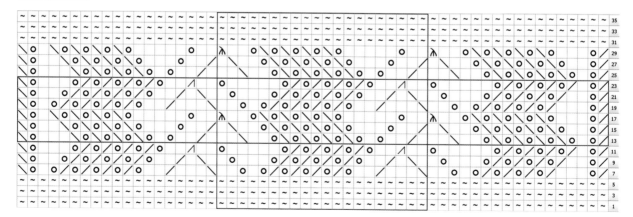

Naomi Pullover

Knitting symbol explanations for the charts can be found on page 23.

DIFFICULTY LEVEL

毛糸 毛糸 毛糸

Finished Size

Adjustable

Materials

→ Schoppel Life Style (100% merino wool; 339 yd/310 m per 3.5 oz/100 g); in #990 White, total depends on finished size: approx. 984.3 yd (900 m), 10.2 oz (290 g) for a long-sleeve sweater in size US 6/8; 1,367 yd (1,250 m), 14.2 oz (403 g) for a long-sleeve sweater in size US 12/14 (yarn comes in 1.75 oz/50 g skeins; you will need 6 [9] skeins for sizes above; estimate as needed for other sizes)

→ Circular knitting needle, US size 6 or 7 (4.0 or 4.5 mm)

→ Crochet hook in the same size

Gauge Swatch

For this pattern, a gauge swatch is not necessary since increases are worked until the desired size has been reached.

Construction Note

The Naomi Pullover sweater is worked in top-down raglan construction. All stitches (Sleeve – Front – Sleeve – Back) are cast on and worked together in one piece. The arrows in the schematic show the direction of work.

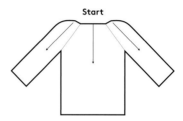

At the transitions between Sleeves and Body, in every other round, 2 stitches each are increased, meaning every other round will have 8 stitches more. The increases are accounted for in the chart.

Chart A

23 21 19 17 15 13 11 9 7 5 3 1

|1|

11 stitches per sleeve.
widthwise pattern repeat: work once

|1|

31 stitches each for Front and Back.
widthwise pattern repeat: work 3 times

INSTRUCTIONS

Beginning & Yoke

Cast on 88 stitches. The number |1| indicates the raglan line stitch.

31		1		11		1		31		1		11		1	
Back		1		Sleeve		1		Front		1		Sleeve		1	

Join in the round, and then knit one round.
After this, continue from Chart A. Only pattern rounds are shown in the chart. In even-numbered rounds, knit all stitches. The framed area shows the widthwise pattern repeat. Due to space constraints, only one Sleeve is shown, and the Body only once, which means that the chart must be worked 2 times in every round. Work Rounds 5 through 24 a total of 3 times. With every repeat of Rounds 5 through 24, in each Sleeve, in the Body, and in the Front, two more repeats of the widthwise pattern repeat will be created. For sizes 18 and larger, repeat Rounds 5 through 24 once more.

IMPORTANT
It is strongly recommended to mark each raglan line stitch with a stitch marker. In Rounds 1, 13, and 21, the raglan line stitch is a **V** (2 stitches). In the respective next round, the yarn over between the **V** will become the new raglan line stitch.

TIP
In regular intervals, a lifeline should be inserted (see page 12).

NOTE ABOUT LARGER SIZES
The raglan line (the 1 stitch between Body and Sleeves) for size US 12/14 should be approx. 10.6 in (27 cm) long. For larger sizes, this line will automatically become longer. However, the raglan line should not turn out too long, which would result in a too wide (and, therefore, too deep) armhole. If this is the case, a larger number of stitches (1 widthwise pattern repeat = 10 stitches more) will be cast on using the backward-loop cast-on method. More about this in the next section.

Main Part (Body)

Now work Rounds 25/26, see Chart B.
The previous rounds, which have been worked earlier, are shown here again for better orientation—do not work them again here.

After having completed Round 26, the sleeve stitches are transferred to a stitch holder or piece of waste yarn for holding and not worked at this time. The raglan line stitches are added to the Body sections.

> **PLEASE NOTE**
> I recommend using a thick piece of yarn in a contrasting color for holding the sleeve stitches.

In place of the now-held sleeve stitches, in Round 27, cast on 3 new underarm stitches each between Front and Back as well as Back and Front by using the backward-loop cast-on method.

> **PLEASE NOTE**
> For larger sizes, instead of 3 stitches, 13 or 23 stitches can be cast on using the backward-loop cast-on method, to prevent the raglan line from becoming too long. In this case, one or two more repeats of the widthwise pattern repeat (10 stitches) will be worked later.

The total stitch count should be a multiple of 10. From here on, work Front and Back together in one piece in the round.
Continue from Chart C, starting with Round 27. The previous rounds, which have been worked earlier, are shown here again for better orientation—do not work them again here.
"+ 3" (or 13 or 23, respectively) are the new underarm stitches in place of the held sleeve stitches.

Repeat Rounds 29 through 33 until the piece is approx. 7.9 in (20 cm) shorter than the desired garment length.

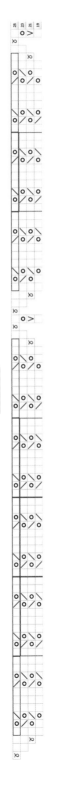

Chart B

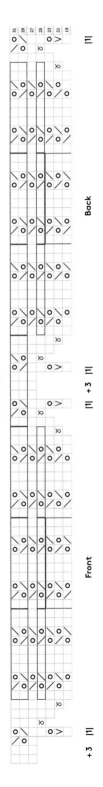

Chart C

Chart D

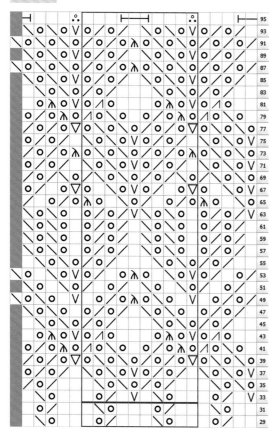

Edge Section in Lace Pattern

Continue from Chart D, working Rounds 33 to 95. Rounds 29/31, which have been worked in the previous chart, are shown here again for orientation—do not work them again.

Move the beginning of the round 2 stitches to the right. The framed area (10 stitches wide) shows the widthwise pattern repeat; repeat it around as often as the stitch count permits.

SPECIAL INSTRUCTIONS FOR THE BEGINNING/END OF THE ROUND
In Rounds 35, 39, 65, 69, 73, and 77, make sure that the yarn over ends up exactly in the middle between the two stitches that had been increased in the preceding pattern round **V**.

In Rounds 49, 53, 87, and 91, knit together the last stitch of the round with the first stitch of the previous round by working "skp."

In Row 95, bind off all stitches with either 1 or 3 chains in between (see pages 14 and 15). This sometimes involves crocheting 3 stitches off ⊢⊒ together. For ⸫, a chain of 3 is additionally worked between the bind-off stitches.

→
CONTINUED

Sleeves

The Sleeves are worked in the round; in even-numbered rounds, all stitches are knitted.

Take up the previously held sleeve stitches, and place them on the needle.

Work 5 stitches into the corresponding additionally cast-on underarm stitches at the body. (Please note for larger sizes: If at the Body, 13 or 23 stitches had been previously cast on between Front and Back / Back and Front, 15 or 25 stitches need to be worked into the corresponding cast-on underarm stitches.)

Start beginning of round exactly in the middle of the additionally cast-on underarm stitches. Continue the stitch pattern over all stitches.

Continue from Chart E, working Round 27 as follows: work 3 stitches into the corresponding cast-on underarm stitches, work over the formerly held sleeve stitches, kfb.

Round 25, which has been worked earlier, is shown here again for better orientation—do not work it again.

Chart E

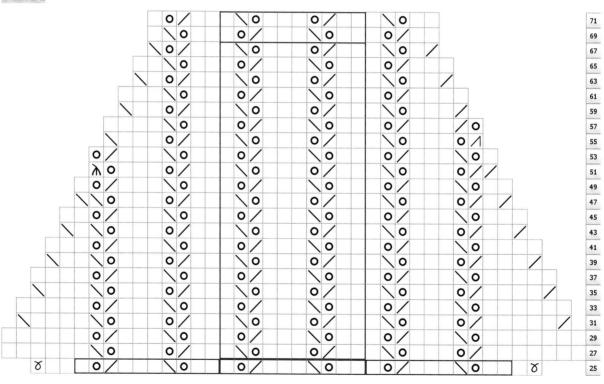

In every 5th round, at the beginning and the end of the round, knit 2 stitches together, until the stitch count is a multiple of 10, which could be, for example, 50 or 60 stitches. Repeat Rounds 69 through 72, until the sleeve is approx. 7.9 in (20 cm) shorter than the desired length.

Lower Sleeve in Lace Pattern

Continue from Chart F, working Round 73.
Rounds 69/71, which have been worked in the previous chart, are shown here again for orientation—do not work them again.
The framed area shows the widthwise pattern repeat; repeat it around as often as the stitch count permits.

Chart F

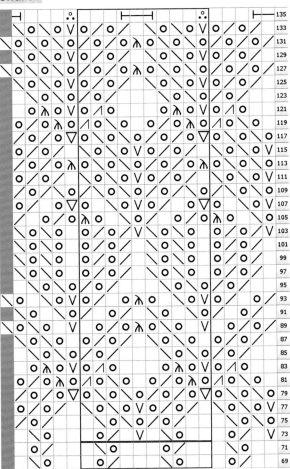

SPECIAL INSTRUCTIONS FOR THE BEGINNING/END OF THE ROUND
In Rounds 75, 79, 105, 109, 113, and 117, make sure that the yarn over ends up exactly in the middle between the two stitches that had been increased in the preceding pattern round **V**.

In Rounds 89, 93, 127, and 131, knit together the last stitch of the round with the first stitch of the previous round by working "skp."

In Round 135, bind off all stitches with either 1 or 3 chains in between (see pages 14 and 15). This sometimes involves crocheting 3 stitches off ⊢━━⊣ together. For ⬚, a chain of 3 is additionally worked between the bind-off stitches.

Finishing

Finish the neckline by adding a crocheted edging as follows: 1 round single crochet, 1 round reverse single crochet.
After the ends have been woven in, soak the Pullover in lukewarm water, gently press out excess water. Block, lightly opening up the lace.

About the Author

Born in 1962, Birgit Freyer still belongs to the generation in which girls received "proper" needlework training as part of the school curriculum. However, it is not a secret that she did not exactly enjoy needlework class in school—a mere potholder earned her an "unsatisfactory," the German equivalent of an "F."

At age 15, she started vocational training in the creative field, followed by studying design in college. Later, she worked as freelance web designer and lecturer in adult education.

She rediscovered knitting 20 years ago. As she always knitted items from her own creative ideas and was constantly asked by friends for patterns, she began to document them by drawing charts—this is how the first few of her patterns came to be. Since then, she has been offering patterns for 15 years at www.die-wolllust.de.

Thanks

I would like to thank all the knitters who have tested and improved the samples for this book: Sylvia Ludwig, Andrea Lindenberg, Ingrid de Moll, Christine Springer, Uta Agbara, Marion Schönsee, Gabriele Meyer-Hermann, Petra Arnhold, Caroline Eckhoff, Almut and Marianne Gothe.

A special thank you goes to Daniela Hoffmann, who not only knitted a few samples but also was closely involved in the creation of this book.

I would also like to thank my husband, Martin Freyer, who shouldered a lot of responsibilities while I worked on this book.

I would further like to thank my parents, Sonja and Manfred Dreier, who made a professional career in this field possible for me.

Last but not least, I would like to express my thanks to companies—Schoppel, Lanartus, and Lang Yarns—that provided yarn support for some of the samples.

You can find the yarn for all designs in my online shop at **www.die-wolllust.de**.